Miscellaneous Records of Jackson County Georgia

- 1780-1858 -

Compiled By:
Joseph T. Maddox & Mary Carter

Southern Historical Press, Inc.
Greenville, South Carolina

This volume was reproduced
from a personal copy located in
the Publishers private library

All rights reserved. No part of this publication may be reproduced,
stored in a retrieval system, transmitted in any form, posted
on the web in any form or by any means without the
prior written permission of the publisher.

Please direct all correspondence and book orders to:
SOUTHERN HISTORICAL PRESS, Inc.
1071 Park West Blvd.
Greenville, SC 29611

ISBN #978-1-63914-678-9
Printed in the United States of America

FOREWORD

Jackson, the 22nd, Georgia county, was so declared as such by an Act of the Legislature February 11, 1796. It was created from Franklin, the ninth county in Georgia, having been established February 25, 1785, following Cherokee Indian cessation May 3, 1783 and the Creek Tribe Nov. 1, 1783.

JACKSON County is indeed important to researchers who seek information about the earlier people of Georgia. First and foremost, is the manner in which records were systematically entered in court house books and maintained down thru the years.

Not only did county officials begin immediately after formation, but they had the forethought to call for records from adjacent counties that predated the formation of Jackson. That is, those records that would affect the people of Jackson County.

Much of Franklin County lands had been previously awarded as bounties for military service. Moreover, Jackson was located near other counties created previously. In the process of expansion brought about by the heavy influx of new people, property turnovers were many. They not only came from counties already established in Georgia, but from the Carolinas, Virginia and Maryland as well.

The records in this booklet contains: Will abstracts, administratorships, guardianships, property deeds and many other records vital to a county and its people.

The information was first copied for Mr. John Ladson, Jr. of Vidalia, Georgia. Mr. Ladson has contributed much in the field of genealogy. He, in turn, made these records available for use in Georgia Pioneers, a quarterly magazine, published by Mrs. Mary Carter of Albany Georgia.

To avoid long hours of searching through various issues of Georgia Pioneers, Mrs. Carter and I agreed it would be handy and useful if these records could be made composite with an index added. So that is what has been done.

Joseph T. Maddox
Irwinton, Georgia 31042

Mary Carter
Albany Georgia 31702

MISCELLANEOUS RECORDS JACKSON COUNTY GEORGIA

Nov. 6th, 1790. Hines Holt of Hancock County, to P e t e r Leeth of Washington County, land in Franklin County granted to ___Call, sold for taxes. Test Ro. Holt J.P., Joseph L. Freeman.

Nov. 10th, 1798. Peter Leath of Warren County, J o h n Marcus of Washington County, 8,000 acres granted in name of Richard Call, on Oconee River in 1786 for $500. Test. Benjamin Gilbert, James Gayne and William West.

July 5, 1798. John H. Foster, T.C., for Wilkes County, to Thomas Terrell for Mary Montgomery, land on Barber's Creek. Test. Robert Carter, ___Derricott, J.P.

___1799, Agreement. Samuel Gardner, Alexander Gardner, to Johnson Strong, to make good any deficiency of title made by John Gordham in his life to said Strong. Test. Richard Bailey.

Mar. 30, 1799. Stephen Collins of Columbia County, to Johnson Strong of Jackson County, formerly Franklin on Oconee River, in the Reserved Fork, originally granted to Stephen Collins, Dec. 7, 1784. Test. John Tindell, Richard Shackleford.

May 2nd, 1799. John Barnett to Johnson Strong, land in the Continental Bounty Reserve, originally granted to Stephen Collins, 1798. Test. David McCleskey.

June 8, 1799. John Strong to Thomas McCoy, 427 acres on Big Creek, conveyed to said Strong by Jeffrey E a r l y in 1798. Test. William Strong, J.P.

John Strong to John Thompson, part of tract conveyed to said Strong by Jeffrey Early to said Strong. Test. William Strong, J.P.

April 2nd, 1798. Daniel Head and wife, Elizabeth, to Micajah Williamson, 250 acres, originally granted to Benjamin Knox, 1787. Test. John Wooten, Wm. Head.

Hezekiah Terrell, Sheriff of Franklin County, to Thomas Hill of Jackson County, a certain t r a c t originally granted to Josiah Woods, sold as the property of Enoch Hodges. Test. M . Williamson, John Martin.

Oct. 17, 1799. Paul Patrick Sr., to his grandson, Paul Patrick, a black mare with blaze face a n d white hind feet: "That I received of James Hathorn this date." Test David Neil, James Hathorn.

Feb. 13, 1798. Isham Matthews of Pendleton District S.C., to William Carter of Jackson County, part of tract originally granted to Daniel Burksdall. Test. Alexander Morrison, J.P. Daniel Matthews.

Sept. 7, 1790. William Hopkins and Micajah Benge to John Stroud, land on Barbers Creek. Test. A. Bankston, J.P., George Hunter.

Mar. 25, 1791. r/ June 2, 1791. Solomon Ellis and wife, Mary, sell to Seakin Dorsey for ₤50, 200 acres originally granted to William Maddox and sold to him by said Ellis.

s/ Mar. 24th, 1791. r/ July 30th, 1791. Same principals, for ₤100 sterling, 92 acres, laid off for Joshua Fuller, and sold by him to said Ellis. Grant originally contained 100 acres, but eight acres sold to Jacob Darsey by Ellis.

s/ Mar. 1, 1790. r/ Aug. 1, 1791. Henry Candler to Thomas Cowan, for ₤4, 6s, 8p, lawful money, sells 26 acres granted to said Candler by Governor Telfair. Bounded by Stanford and Duncan lands.

s/ July 30, 1785. r/ Aug. 2, 1791. Jas. Graves, of Wilkes County, planter, sells to Michael Griffin for ₤40, 200 acres on south side of Little River, granted to Graves by Sir James Wright ESQUIRE, Capt. General and Commander-in-Chief of our own Province. Patent dated April 2, 1770.

s/ and r/ Aug. 6th, 1791. Deed of gift, Robert Burton, to son, Caleb, 300 acres adjacent own property, one cow named Lady one cow named Blossom; one cow named Motley and old Gentle's youngest heifer, all their increase from the year 1792. Also one bed, all the cloathes thereto, one pewter basin and dish, one iron pot, etc.

Same principals and date, sells for ₤40 250 acres on Reedy Creek.

s/ AND r/ Aug. 6, 1791. Thomas Smythe, Jr., now of Queen Ann's County Maryland, to Richard Footman of the City of Philadelphia, merchant, for ₤500, current money, of the State of Maryland, two tracts of land, purchased from Daniel Sturgis, Sept. 3, 1790. No acreage given.

s/ and r/ Aug. 23, 1791. Deed of gift. Thomas Hamilton to beloved wife, Concord, all and singular, my goods and chattels, being my dwelling house, together with Dr. Edmond Dillon's bond and mortgage, dated Feb. 26, 1789; also Robert Montgomery's for Jan. 18th, 1790. Also Negroes Hercules, yellow color, 20 years old. Nego fellow "Hope", yellow, 18. Woman "Rinch", 17, and her daughter Betty, born March 14th, last, and a girl Sue, age 12. Also 800 acres of land on both sides of the Trading Road - 3 different tracts - and 700 acres of Little Kiokee. One black gelding; all my stock of cattle and hogs; in trust with Isaiah Wright. (He was Concord's brother).

s/ Jan. 15th, 1791. r/ Aug. 21st, 1791. Jacob Goar, and wife, Rachael, to William Booker, for ₤70, current money, 100 acres on Little Kiokee Creek, bounded by Youngblood, Gideon Booker, William Zachry and conveyed to said Goar by said John Youngblood by deed devised in Richmond County.

s/ Jan. 15th, 1791. r/ Aug. 23rd, 1791. John Wright and his wife Alcea, to Thomas Cowan for ₤15, sell 69 acres, part of a 95 acre tract granted to said Wright by Governor Telfair Dec. 4, 1790.

s/ June 4, 1791. r/ June 25, 1795. John Lamar and wife, Lucy, of Richmond County, to Joel Jones, for ₤10, 50 acres "beginning at the north corner of a tract granted to Leonard Marbury, bounded on the east by Kelly's Branch.

Same dates and grantor as above. To Isaac Cliett, for ₤10, 64 acres adjacent to above tract.

s/ May 21st, 1795. r/ June 20, 1795. Francis Hornsby and wife, Nancy, of Richmond County to Samuel Hanson, for ₤35, 200 acres on Uchee Creek, part of Original grant to Gabriel Erchart.

s/ Apr. 7, 1795. r/ June 26, 1795. Jas. Hamilton, Sheriff, on writ of fi-fa. (On suit of John Cobbison), auction off property of Moses Marshall and John Doss(?) John L. Dixon, purchaser, for ₤23, of 119 acres of Greenbrier Creek adjacent to Basil Jones, Elias Jones, William Beckham and John Cobb's land.

s/ Feb. 6, 1789. r/ June 26, 1795. John Marshall to William Few for ₤10, lawful money sells 100 acres, part of a 225 acre tract granted to said John, Jan. 7, 1786.

s/ July 2, 1795. r/ same date. Appointment of Trustees, Anthony Haynes, "in consideration of the confidence I have in friends Thomas Haynes, Esq. and David Maxwell," put all the property left in his will to Chaney, colored woman and her eight children, in trust with the above named.

s/ Dec. 13, 1783. r/ July 2, 1795. Benjamin Wells and wife Mary, for ₤80, sell to William Few.300 acres on both sides of Greenbrier Creek and on north fork of great Kiokee Creek. Originally granted to said Wells by King George the Third. Feb. 5, 1770. (William Few Jr.)

s/ Dec. 10, 1788. r/ July 3, 1795. Wm. Barnett, Esq. Sheriff of Richmond County to William Few Jr. on a judgement against James Brown, deceased, for ₤277, 17s, 8p, a tract of 700 acres originally granted to Richard Williamson May 1st, 1770, conveyed to said Brown by deed June 1, 1770 Sold at auction and purchased by Few for ₤-200.

s/ Mar. 22, 1780. r/July 9, 1795. Jacob Castleberry, blacksmith, and wife Mary, to Samuel Johnston for ₤50, 100 acres on White Oak Creek, granted to said Castleberry.

s/ Feb. 22nd, 1795. r/ July 15th, 1795. Eddmond B. Jenkins, of Richmond County to Thomas Glascock, Esq. for five shillings, sells 40,000 acres in Columbia County bounded on all sides by lands vacant at time of survey. Granted in four separate tracts by Gov. George Matthews, Esq. Oct. 2nd, 1794 to said Jenkins. Also 200 acres in Columbia County, bounded on N. E. by

James Danelly. S. W. by Richard Call. S. E. by Headstall Creek, Jan. 29th, and 2,000 acres on Wilkes County line granted Jenkins Oct. 2nd, 1790. (At the time Wilkes and Richmond had a common boundary, north south and west, until the formation of Columbia County in 1790.)

s/ Mar. 17th, 1790. r/ Apr. 10th, 1795. Alexander Steele and wife Fanny of Wilkes County to Charles Reynolds for ₤50, 100 acres on Germany Creek bounded S. W. by Dunn, S. E. by T. Ricketson, S.E. by Cooper.

s/ Oct. 22nd, 1792. r/ Apr. 14, 1795. Isham Bayliss and his wife Betsy to Randall Ramsey, Jr. for ₤135, two tracts 105 acres granted to Robert Graves Oct. 4th, 1774 on Little River, also 30 acres adjacent former, conveyed by Robert Whitten to us.

s/ Jan. 24th, 1795. r/ Apr. 14th, 1795. Joseph Mooney and his wife Hannah, and his mother Mary Mooney from Newberry S.C. sell to Aaron Parkes for ₤50, 175 acres on west side of Upton Creek, part of 550 acre tract granted to Joseph Mooney, Sr., July 3, 1770. (Mooneys were Quakers)

s/ Oct. 6, 1794. r/ Apr. 15, 1795. John Ganley to John Duke for ₤25, 100 acres on Great Kiokee Creek.

s/ June 15th, 1793. r/ Apr. 16th, 1795. David Murray, Jr. and wife Mary, from Wilkes County to Aquilla Howard for ₤270 350 acres originally granted to Isaac Jackson July 3, 1770, by Sir James Wright by said Jackson and conveyed to Henry Wright May 16, 1773 by him conveyed to David Murray Dec. 1, 1790.

s/ Dec. 5th, 1787. r/ Apr. 16th, 1795. William Hickson and wife Elizabeth, to Jonothan Motes, both of Wrightsboro Township, for ₤500, 200 acres on waters of Upton Creek, being part of 400 acres granted to William Hickson July 4th, 1769 by Sir James Wright.

s/ Apr. 5, 1790. r/ Apr. 16, 1795. Eli Garrett to John Eubanks, "in consequence of a free gift to him before the sealing of these presents," 95 acres on Kegg Creek adjacent ot Griffith's pond.

s/ Dec. 13th, 1795. r/ Apr. 1795. Chas. Reynolds and wife Mary, to John Langston for ₤40, 100 acres on Germany Creek formerly belonging to Alex Steele. Also one other tract of 26 acres, part of survey for Geter Carter.

s/ Oct. 16th, 1787. r/ same date. Power of Attorney from Sarah Webster, seamstress of Lancaster County, S. C. to son-in-law, John Fleming to recover all sums due her.

s/ Mar. 2nd, 1790. I, Thomas Meriwether for ₤65, do forever set at liberty, emancipate and convey a full right of liberty and freedom to a certain Micah Coley, alias Quash, and her offspring.

s/ Mar. 2, 1790. r/ Apr. 20, 1795. Bill of sale from Jeremiah Lamkin and John Lamkin, six Negroes: Molly, Lucy, Silva, Selah and Ben for ₤200.

Oct. 6, 1806. Last will of William Allen produced and proven.

Jan. 6th, 1807. George Haynie, adm. in right of his wife on estate of Jeremiah Holliday, makes returns.

Last will of Michael Borders produced and proved.

Last will of Henry Walker produced and proved by William Willis and James McDonald.

Wiley Ross and Abraham Venable appointed guardians of Martin, Fanny, Nancy and John Morton Holliday, heirs of Jeremiah Holliday, deceased, and they are authorized to receive from George Haynie, Adm. of Jeremiah Holliday, deceased, in right of his wife, Margaret Haynie, all the estate, etc.

Sarah and Garrett W. Parks, Adms. of estate of James Parks, deceased, ask to sell 250 acres of land on Cabin Creek for benefit of heirs, etc. Granted.

May 4, 1807. Ann Holmes appointed guardian to Mary and Safronia Holmes, minors and orphans of James Holmes.

Last will of Daniel Evans, late of this county, deceased, produced and proven by John and Jacob Gerrard. (not of record).

James Clark appointed guardiam of Patsy Clark, minor and orphan of John Clark, deceased.

On the information of Thomas Hanson, that Mildred Cooper, a girl about 14, resident of this county and orphan has only $16.00 for her support and without a home. John Watterson agrees to take her if she can be bound to him. Ordered that she be bound for the term of four years, beginning April 6th, last.

James Alford praying that good titles be given to 220 acres lying in Franklin County when surveyed, now Clarke County, being a part of grant to Micajah Williamson, Sr. and inherited by Micajah, Jr. who failed to make titles...Granted.

Jemima Lovejoy, William Lovejoy and JETHRO Mobley appointed Adms. of estate of Edward Lovejoy, deceased.

Thomas, Jane and James Shields obtain letters of Adm. on estate of Patrick Shields, deceased.

June 1st, 1807. George N. Lyles obtains letter of Adm. on estate of Leonard Marbury.

July 7, 1807. Last will of George Bagby deceased, produced and proven by William and Delilah Pentecost.

Nov. 2, 1807. It being represented to this court that William, Lewis, John and Nancy Ezzard, four children of John Ezzard, have been abandoned for some years by their father. Two eldest bound to Robert Johnson, two youngest bound to Edward Adams.

Jonothan Poulson, orphan about 13 years old, bound to Thomas Castleberry. Mark Poulson, brother to Jonothan, about 11 years old, bound to William Shipp.

Jan. 4th, 1808. Last will of William Headen, produced and proven.

Abraham Venable and Wiley Ross make returns as guardians of orphans of Jeremiah Holliday.

Feb. 1st, 1808. Lewis Crow, orphan of Jacob Crow, chose Isaac Reed as guardian Court appoints Isaac guardian of Jacob Crow, Jr.

Ezekiel Ralston obtains letter of Adm. on estate of Isaac Wright.

Unity Rogers obtains letter of adm. on estate of Benjamin Rogers.

Joseph J. Scott obtains letter of adm. on estate of Doct. Thomas Carson.

Mar. 7, 1808. Polly Williams, daughter of Isaac Williams, abandoned by both father and mother, bound to Wiley Ross.

William Cates, adm. of John Berry, deceased, inhuman treatment to orphans, ordered to give them up.

William Hendley ordered to support his wife Jane Hendley. Thos. Camp, Esq. appt. her guardian.

Adms. of Thomas Rogers, deceased, ordered to appear at next court because of mismanagement.

Mar. 15, 1808. Court held for settling with the adms. of Thomas Rogers and John Berry, Deceased...Settled.

Apr. 4th, 1808. William Ship, sec. for Elizabeth Kirkland, admx. of William Kirkland, deceased, prays to be relieved ....Granted.

John Carmichael, Robert Morgan and Polly Morgan, obtain letters of adm. on estate of Thomas Morgan, deceased.

Elizabeth Cook and James Clark obtain letters of adm. estate of Jonothan Cook, deceased.

John Hobson obtains letter of adm. on estate of Duncan Campbell, deceased.

Thomas Hyde obtains letter of adm. on estate of Robert Hyde, deceased.

MISCELLANEOUS RECORDS JACKSON COUNTY GEORGIA

Daniel Johnson and Peleg Rogers make returns as Adms. estate Thomas Rogers, deceased. Sale of land and slaves.

Hugh Montgomery and Samuel Gardner appt.. guardians to orphans of Thomas Rogers, dec. to-wit: David Rogers, Thos. Stanfer Rogers, Mary Rogers and John Henderson Rogers.

WILL. David Dickson. s/ June 5, 1808, p/ Nov 7, 1808. Sons: James, William and Samuel Dickson. To daughter Betsy Baily, whatever is due me from Robert Baily. Daughter, Mattie Beatty, a note on Francis Beatty. Nephew Dickson Baily. Exrs. Nephew David Dickson and Elijah Cowan. Esq. Test. Alexander Gillespie and Sarah Gillespie.

WILL. William Morgan. s/Apr. 26, 1809. p/ May 1st, 1809. "Low state of health" Wife Priscilla. Sons; Blake, William and Jesse Morgan. Daughters: Patsy Shepherd, Joice Morgan; three youngest daughters: Priscilla, Esther and Mahala Morgan. "when Priscilla becomes of age." Exrs. Wife Priscilla and Samuel Hay. Test: James Rogers, Ephraim Patrick, David Tuttle.

WILL. Phillip Avary. s/ Jan. 18, 1809. p/ July 3, 1809. Wife Betsy. Daughters: Betsy and Rebecca. Sons: William and Thomas Avary. Exrs. Wife and two sons. Test. James Hamilton. Johnson Frost.

WILL. Nicholas Hobson. s/ Mar. 7, 1809. p/ May 1st, 1809. Wife Sally. Sons: Wm., John, Matthew, Baker, Christopher, Francis and Allen Hobson. Daughters Jimmy Smith, Polly, Patsy and Agnes Hobson. Exrs. John, Matthew and Baker Hobson. Test. George Hampton and Job Rogers.

WILL. Jacob Pettijohn. s/ Dec.13, 1810 Wife Betsy. $5.00 and her support out of certain Negroes as long as she continues a widow & conducts herself as a Mother. Sons: James, Reuben, William and Abram. Daughter Sally Kirkpatrick. Nephew: Fleming Staten (Slaton?). Sons Reuben, Abram, Warren (?) and Hugh Montgomery Executors. Test: George Doss and Joseph Cunningham.

WILL. John Morris. s/ June 27, 1810. p/ Mar. 4th, 1811. Wife Elizabeth. Sons: Zachariah and Jesse Morris. Daughters: Polly Duke; Sally and Susannah Morris, when they come of age. Wife Elizabeth, Frederick Thompson and Eli Whaley, Exrs. Test: Joseph Camp and Wm. Nichols.

WILL. Samuel Haggard. s/ Aug. 30, 1810 p/ June 3rd, 1811. Wife Ruth, "to my beloved children as follows": John, Jas., Samuel Jr., Jonothan, George and Susannah Haggard; Patsy Smith, Elizabeth Freemond, Anna Hix, Sarah Brown; Frances Hardy and Hannah Cook, $1.00 each. To my youngest sons, Frank and Alford Haggard, all my estate at my wife's death. Exrs. Jesse Bennett and Thomas Perry. Test. Solomon Stevens and Reves Bruzel.

WILL. Henry Snow (Farmer). s/ Apr. 7th, 1810. p/ May 1st, 1811. "All my property to Mark Snow and Mark's wife, Elizabeth," All my other heirs I cut off as the State directs." Mark Snow and wife, Elizabeth, Executors. John C. Watkins; Joel and Margart. Jelton, Test.

WILL. Joseph Shields. s/ Mar. 13, 1818. p/ May 4th, 1818. Wife Peggy. Son James. Daughter Jane Thurmond. Son-in-law Thos. Thurmond; son-in-law Matthew Wiley. G-son John Ragains. Son James and Elijah Oliver Executors. Test. John Boring, Levi Lowry, J.P.

WILL. John Scisson. s/ Mar. 15th, 1818. p/ Sept. 6, 1818. Wife Susannah. Daughter Charlotte "to be educated". Robert Hemphill and Jas. Scisson, Exrs. Test. Sabry Hemphill and Vardary Scisson.

WILL. James Allison. s/ Feb. 9th, 1818. p/ Jan. 4, 1819. Wife Ealinor. Children: Paschal M., Lucia Oraline, Samuel Wilson, and James Seaborn Allison. Exrs. Wife, Ealinor and Samuel Wilson. Test: Obediah Waton. James McElhannan and Josiah Watson

WILL. Thomas Stpry. s/ Oct. 22nd, 1819. p/ ,ay 15th, 1820. Wife Christian. Minor children - names not given. Wife Christian and brother Edward Story, exrs. Test: John Harrison, Ann B. Gates, Elisha Gates.

WILL. David Henderson. s/ Jan. 18,1821. p/ Feb. 2, 1821. Beloved wife, afflicted son, Robert. Other children: John D.B., Jeremiah William, Robert Scott Thomas Henderson and Hannah Ann, Tabitha Elizabeth Jane Henderson. Brother-in-law Baly Chandler and Bartley Montgomery, Exrs. Test: Polly Freeman, B. Mayo. John Boring

WILL. Samuel Barnett, Sr. s/ June 20th, 1819. p/ Sept. 3rd, 1821. Wife Margaret, Son Samuel. Test. Russell Jones, William Appleby, Stephen Potts, John J. Parks.

WILL. Thomas Johnson. s/ Sept. 13,1821. p/ Nov. 17th, 1821. Wife Mary. Son Daniel Merrill. Son Stephen. Son William. Daughter Sally Trapp. Six children (no other names given)(Stephen was medical student) Exrs. Hugh Montgomery, Edward Adams and Joseph Davis. Test: Polly Ratchford, Edward Adams and Charles Smith.

WILL. Lewis Barker. s/ Mar. 10th, 1818. p/ May. 6, 1822. Children: Patsy Parsons, Isham Barker, Sally Polk. Gray Barker; Lewis Barker, Polly Phillips, Cillar Polk, Eldridge Barker; Urvil (?) Barker(dau), Exrs. Parks Chandler and Isham Lewis; Gray and Eldridge Barker. Test: James Hemphill, Abraham Powell, Joseph Davis.

WILL. Samuel Wilson. s/ Nov. 20, 1818. p/ Jan. 8th, 1822. Wife Lucy. Single daughters: Mary Lucy, Jane and Caroline, all under 21. Sons: Samuel, William and John. John, youngest, under age. Daughters: Eleanor Allison. Sarah Seay, Ann(?) Bery? Daughter Lydia. Wife Lucy and son Samuel, Exrs. Test: Charles Venable, William D. Martin and A. Lawhorn.

WILL. Prosser Horton. s/ Nov. 29, 1820. p/ Mar. 29, 1823. Wife Sarah. Sons: Fletcher and Prosser Horton. Daughter Feraby Horton, deceased son William Horton. Daughter Sarah Glenn. Son-in-law Washington Allen. Exrs. James Hemphill and William Bell. Test: Chas. Dougherty, E. Price, John Todd and John Young.

WILL. John Lambert. s/ June 6, 1826. p/ July 4, 1826. Wife Sarah. To son Alexander Brazeal, alias Lambert. Son John Brazeal, alias Lambert. To son, Edward Lambert, all the land je lives on. Exrs. wife Sarah, Edwin Lambert, Washington Brazeal, alias Lambert and John Flanigan.. Test: John Matterson?, Rachael Pentecost, Matthew M. Pentecost, William Brazeal.

WILL. Phillip Ryan Sr. s/ 1821. p/ July 2nd, 1822. Wife Obedience, life estate to dispose of to such of my children or grand children as she thinks best. To granddaughters Susannah Lumpkin and Sarah Nance, $50.00 each. My wife, Obedience Ryan, my _____? Whited Ryan, William Matthews and Thomas Mitchell, exrs. Test: John Creighton and Elizabeth Creighton.

WILL. Obediah Watson. s/ Sept. 22,1829. p/ Jan. 12,1830. To my wife, life estate, to go to children of my brother, Joseph Watson. Exrs. Joseph Watson and Joseph Landrum. Test: Samuel A. Wilson, Charles Tapp and Glenn Phelps.

WILL. John Carmichael. s/ Aug. 29,1822. p/ Oct. 15, 1822. Grandson, John Carmichael Jr. son of Duncan Carmichael. If said Duncan does not come and make application for his part of the lot before said John Carmichael comes of age, Duncan's part to be paid to John. Daughter Satah Styles All money arising from sales to be divided among my lawful heirs. Exr. John Carmichael. Test: Isaac York, Sion Pritchett and Abner McGuire.

WILL. Josiah H. Baugh. s/ Nov. 18,1822. p/ Mar. 23, 1823. Wife Sarah and son Daniel, sole heirs and Exrs. Test: Moses Wilson, T.M.Wilson; Thomas Staplet, W.H. Pittman. CODICIL: My other nine children, to-wit: Nancy Sheppard; Mrs. (?) Foster, Jane Harper, Sarah Deel, Esther Harper, Catherine Purdom, Barrtley Baugh, Jeremiah Baugh and Henry M. Baugh.

WILL. John McElhannon, Sr. s/ May 15th, 1834. p/ July 7,1834. Wife Eleanor. Sons: Hugh, Cooper, James, John, Christopher, Isaiah, Hezekiah, FRANCIS a n d Steward. Daughters: Elinor Bell, Elizabeth McMurty Unity Potts and Peggy Shields. Grandson: Francis McElhannon. Exrs. Hezekiah, Francis and Hugh McElhannon. Test: Nancy A. Watson, Cammy Arnold, Stephen Arnold.

WILL. William Williamson. s/ Dec. 17, 1832. p/ Nov. 3rd, 1834. Nephews: James Williamson McCleskey, Eusebius McCleskey Madison West McCleskey, Milton T. McCleskey. Nieces: Margaret McCleskey, M a r y McCleskey, Elizabeth McCleskey, land known as the Horton tract. Nephews: James Moon, Jackson Moon, Hartwell Moon, Robert Moon. Elizabeth Moon, Betsy Moon, land drawn by Boler Moon, whose chances I h a v e bought in the present lottery. Sisters: Jinny Doss, life estate to lot No. 376, 7th, District Gwinnett County. Sally Moon, life estate in slave, Polly McCleskey. Half-brother, James Mitchell, land in the 3rd, District Houston County drawn by Abner Sailors, to be paid by Adam Williamson in annual installments of $50.00. To the children of my sister, Betsy Power?, $300.00, to be paid in equal portions as t h e y arrive at full age. Adam Williamson, Exr. Test: John Park, Phineas Matthews, Henry Crawford.

WILL. Samuel R. Henderson. s/ Dec. 13, 1834. p/ Sept. 17th, 1835. Wife Delilah, my children, some, if not,all under age. Wife Delilah a n d brother, John M. Henderson, Exrs. Test. Elias Henderson, Nathaniel G. Henderson and Ira Foster.

WILL. Jacob Braselton, Sr. s/ Aug. 9, 1835. p/ Nov. 2, 1835. Daughter Rebecca Brazeal. Sons: John, Henry, William, J a c o b, Reuben, Daniel, Job and Amos Braselton. Sons Jacob a n d Reuben Exrs. Test: John Randolph, John H. Randolph, Washington R. Randolph.

WILL. Elizabeth Cunningham. s/ June 9, 1835. p/ June 5,1836. "My three children living today. Joseph T. a n d James Cunningham and Mary Doss. Mentions Lot No. 263, 3rd, District, original Cherokee (263) County, now Floyd County. Grandson John Doss, forced her to sign away this land about May 10th, 1834, when she was so troubled over the death of her son, Andrew Cunningham, Elizabeth, Jane and Sarah Ross, daughters of her daughter M a r y Doss. Edward Story and Joseph T.Cunningham, Executors. Test: John Appleby, Saml Knox and A.G.Story.

WILL. John Roberson. s/ Dec. 27, 1835. p/ July 4th, 1836. Wife Alcey, his two orphaned children, John and Francis Wood to live on with her until they come of age. To nephews, James and William Wood, nephew Henry Smith. Nieces:two daughters of sister ___ Smith, of Franklin County Georgia. Other legatees:Hezekiah, James, William and David Smith and Israel Roberson Smith. Test: John J. Singleton, Wm. Varnum, William Bell.

WILL. Alcy Roberson. s/ Apr. 9, 1836. p/ July 4th, 1836. Nephew: Frederick D. LOWRY. Brothers: John and James Lowry. Sister; Sarah Wimberly. Charles Cheatham (relationship not shown). Children of Sarah Wimberly.James Wimberly afflicted, Charity Miller. Methodist church $500.00 To Frances Wood a n d John Wood, who now live with me, bedstead, etc. To nephew John Wimberly, $1.00. Brother John Lowry Executor. Test. Joseph J. Singleton, Asa Varnum and Anna Varnum.

WILL. James Nash. s/ ? p/ July 4, 1836 W i f e, Margaret. Sons: Reuben, Gabriel a n d William, and the heirs of my son, James N a s h. James to have a life estate. Oldest son, Elijah Nash. Mentions deed of gift to some of the children. Sons Gabriel and Reuben Nash, Exrs. Test. William Thurmond, Caleb D. Riden, Magnus Brooks, J.P.

WILL. Boley Embry. s/ June 16, 1836. p/ July 4, 1836. Wife Unitt(y)? Children: Tempy, Sarah, William L. J o h n Green B., under age. Elizabeth Mattias, Talbot and Hezkiah L., some, if not all, under age. John Embry a n d Lewis Hardy, Exrs. Test. William R. Wellborn, Butler Williams, Martin Anthony.

WILL, Mary Finley. s/ Jan. 21st, 1835. p/ July 5th, 1836. Beloved nephew James Morris, and his sister Mary Hanson, if she be alive at my death, or her heirs. Test: Jos. J. Singleton, Asa Varnum.

WILL, Sarah Trout. s/ Mar. 9th, 1831. p/ Jan. 1837. Granddaughter, Arabella Shaw, sole heir. Test: John Lindsey, Giles Mitchell.

WILL, William Potts. s/ Dec. 28, 1836. p/ Jan. 1837. Wife Mary. Children: Moses Potts, Claiborn Harris, William Nimmens, William Anderson, Thomas Potts and Thos. Henderson, and orphans of Alexander Potts. Test: Meshack T. Wilhite, D. M. Burns, Ludwell Worsham.

WILL, Samuel Knox, Sr. s/ Apr. 28, 1836. p/ Jan. 2, 1837. Wife Mary(Luckie) Daughters: Jane Luckie, Mary Roberston, Ann Jarratt, Cynthia Borders. Sons: Samuel and William Knox who are also Exrs. Test: Joseph T. Cunningham, Andrew Cunningham and Edward Story. (Mary Luckie is said to have been a widow, Samuel was the son of John and Jean Gracy Knox of Ireland.)

WILL, James Tait. s/ Dec. 11, 1836. p/ July 1837. Wife Susannah. Three youngest children: James, Delilah and Mary Tait. To James Garner, land on which Green Garner now lives, which was purchased from George Shaw. Son: James Tait, part of home place. James and George Shields, Exrs. Test: John J. McCullock, William Lyle, Isaac Boring.

WILL, John McCarty. s/ Jan. 16th, 1837. p/ July 1837. Wife Mary, all land, etc., after 40 acres is laid off to son John, son William. Daughters Susannah Thurmond and Belton Thurmond?. To daughter Elizabeth Vinson and George Vinson $5.00. Balance to be divided between son Cornelius and daughter Mary. Cornelius to maintain his mother and sister Mary until she marries. Wife Mary, Excx. Test Polly Garrett, Little Berry Brooks, Magnus Brooks.

WILL, Samuel Street. s/ Apr. 19, 1837. p/ Sept. 1837. Wife Polly. Daughters: Dorcas and Polly Ann, not married. Son William, son Samford. Wife, Polly, sole Exctx. Test: P.A.Pittman, W.M.Gaithright.

WILL, James Glenn. s/ Dec. 2, 1835. p/ Nov. 1837. Wife Elizabeth. Son James R. Glenn. Daughters: Jane, Eunice, Elizabeth, Synthy, and Letitia, $100.00 each. My nine children, viz: Mary, Gober, Jane Rian, John W. Glenn, Joshua N. Glenn, Eunice Sowell, Elizabeth Hampton, Synthy Shockley. James R. Glenn and Letitia Glenn. Sons John W. and Joshua N. Glenn, Exrs. Test: Henry Crawford, James Smith, William D. Smith.

WILL, Hannah PARK. s/ Oct. 16, 1837. p/ Mar. 1838. Son: Russell Park, sole heir and Exr. Test: Thos. Stapler, B.F.Park.

WILL, Sarah Howard. s/ Mar. 30th, 1830. p/ July 1838. Son Hardy Howard, Lot No. 95,250 acres, 27th, District Early County To daughters Elizabeth Sutton? and Hannah Howard, Lot No. 73, 6th, District, Lee County and the home wherein I now live in Jackson County. Test: Gabriel B. Church, Sarah Church, James Williams, J.P.

WILL, Obedience Ryan. s/ May 8th, 1835. p/ Sept. 1838. In obedience to the last will of my late husband, Philip Ryan, deceased, that the Negroes remain on the home plantation under the superintendence of John Nance and Archibald Moon, the proceeds to be applied to the support of my daughter, Elizabeth Hall, and in case of her death, to my son, Whitehead Ryan. To Sarah Dyer, $35.00, a balance of $50 left her by her grandfather. To grandson Westly Nance. To granddaughter Susan Lampkin, such tracts of land as may be drawn by me in the contemplated land Lottery: to grandson Lewis Lampkin, suit of clothes on his 18th, birthday, etc. Mentions land in 20th, District of Early County, drawn by Phillip Ryan. John Nance and Archibald Moon, Exrs. Test: John Parks Samuel Hancock, S.M.Smith.

WILL. James Cochran. p/ 1828. Wife: Mary. Three daughters: Judith Winn, Ann Key and Jane Thurmond. Exrs. Elisha Winn, Tandy Key a n d Harrison Thurmond. Test: Horatio Webb, Peter E. McMillan, Andrew McLane.

REMNANTS OF COURT OF ORDINARY RECORD

1802. Peleg Rogers and Daniel Johnson, in right of his w i f e, formerly Martha Rogers, Executrix of Thos. Rogers, dec'd. made returns.

Ordered that the returns of Jane Kelough admtrx. of t h e estate of John Kelough, be filed in Clerk's Office for examination.

Thomas Hill came before t h e Court and rendered his account as overseer of the poor, which was approved.

Oct. 25th, 1802. Present, same Esquires

James Kelough made returns as Exctrx. of John Kelough, decd. Ordered recorded, except Voucher No. 21.

J a m e s Moore, adm. of Michael Moore, decd. made returns.

Patience a n d Elijah Hendon, Extrs. of Isham Hendon, decd. made returns.

James Stamps, Extr. last will and testament of Timothy Stamps made returns.

Last will and testament of Robert Park, decd. produced and proved, ordered recorded and letters of test. granted according to law.

J o h n Thurmond asks that the adm. of Bartholomew Zachary, decd. be required to give good titles to this land in Greene County. Ditto for Joseph Ratchford to land in Jackson County and the adm. of Richard Moore, Decd.

Jacob Lindsey adm. of I s h a m Strong, made returns.

Jonothan Lane presents account against t he estate of Thomas Rogers, decd. for Negro girl eight years old, and which account is settled by the turning over to said Lane a mare and colt by Peleg Rogers administrator. Test: John Hampton, J.P. Edward Adams, Clerk.

COURT OF ORDINARY. Feb. 10, 1803.

Letter of adm. applied for and granted to Margaret Holliday on the estate of Jeremiah Holliday, late of this county, deceased.

Robert Ellison dismissed as Security on adm. of estate of Robert Campbell, late of this county, deceased.

COURT OF ORDINARY, April 26, 1803. Present: James Pittman, James Hendrix, Wm. Foster.

Letters of adm. granted to Mary Jones on the estate of Thomas J o n e s, late of this county, deceased.

Letters of adm. granted to Solomon Carter on estate of Solomon Carter, late of this county.

The petition of Charles Wakefield that the adm. of Henry Summerall, dec. of Wilkes County, be ordered to give clear titles on 300 acfes of land on Brushy Creek, which Summerall agreed to give by Oct. next, under date of May 2nd, 1790, which was witnessed by Champion Travis Taylor. Granted.

COURT OF ORDINARY July 25, 1802.

Abraham S c o t t and Ann Knox asked for and obtained letters of adm. on the estate of James Knox, late of this county, dec., and that James Croll be added as another adm. at their request.

James Wilson, adm. for John Wilson, dec. made returns.

Margaret Holliday, adm. made returns.

David Kinsey, adm. James Kinsey, dec. made returns.

Solomon Carter prays that James Moore be made joint administrator with him on the estate of Solomon Carter, late of this county, dec. Granted/

Samuel Gardner asks to be dismissed as adm. of the estate of Robert Campbell late of this county, dec. as he has finished GRANTED.

Charles Strickland asks to be relieved as Security for adm. of estate of Henry Strickland, late of this county, dec. and that Daniel Taylor be appointed in his stead. Granted.

William Carter prays to be exonerated as Security on adm. on the estate of Solomon Carter, dec. Granted.

COURT OF ORDINARY, Oct. 29, 1803.

Sarah Durbin applied for and granted letters of adm. on the estate of Luke Durbin, deceased.

Sally Park, Garrett W. Park and John Park, having given necessary citation to ontain letters of adm. on the estate of James Park, dec. They are granted.

Charles Wakefield, prays that the adm. of Henry Summerall give clear title to land lying in Oglethorpe County. Granted.

Jesse McGehee produced the last will and testament of Nathan McGehee. Proved and ordered to be recorded.

Jonothan Pharr applied for and granted letters of adm. on estate of Francis Pharr deceased.

James Stamps, adm. of the estate of Timothy Stamps, makes returns.

Solomon Carter, Jr. adm. of Solomon Carter Sr. is ordered to surrender all bonds, notes, etc. into the hands of Edward Adams Clerk of Court, as Solomon Jr. is said to be about to remove from the State.

Robert Venable appointed guardian of Frances Venable.

COURT OF ORDINARY, Jan. 24, 1804.

Robert Henderson applies for and receive letters of adm. on the estate of Jacob Summerford.

Deborah Moore asks for and granted letters of adm. on the ess tate of Samuel Moore, late of this county, deceased.

Letters of adm. granted to Nathan Camp, and Elizabeth Gideon on the estate of Jas. Gideon, late of this county, deceased.

Ordered that James Moore, one of adm. of Solomon Carter, late of this county, decd. do proceed to act as such and that the Clerk deliver to him all documents, etc. taken from the hands of Solomon Carter, Jr. one of the adm.

Arthur Foster appointed guardian for William Hambrick.

Robert McCord appointed guardian for James McCord, Nancy McCord and Polly McCord, orphans of Abram McCord, decd.

Francis Neal appointed adm. of Jos. Neal

Apr. 6, 1802. Samuel Henderson, adm. of the estate of Robert Campbell, decd. asks to be authorized to make good titles to land. Granted.

Nancy Morris, among others, names not shown, were bound to Mason Ezzard until they reach the age of 18.

Ordered that David Peak be appointed guardian of Candace Peak an illegitimate child of Judith Peak. Also ordered that Jacob Lindsey, the reputed father of this child, pay to said guardian $20.00 a year for four years.

Estate of John Nelson, decd., to Bozeman Adair, dr. for the use of Elinor Nelson, sister of a helpless child.

March 8th, 1800. Supporting a helpless child by name of Francis Nelson, orphan by the name of Francis Nelson, child of said decd. at $60.00 a year. Ditto for years 1801, 1802, 1803. $240.00. Ordered that this amount be allowed Eleanor Nelson, and the adm. settle with her accordingly.

MINUTES OF ORDINARY'S COURT - no date, but probably 1804.

Ordered that Robert, Mary and Elizabeth Berry, orphans of John Berry, decd. be bound to Stephen Brooks, the two girls until they are 18; the boyd until he is 21. They not having any proper persons to take care of them, and the estate not being sufficient for their support. That they be taught to read and write, and the girls be given at least two decent suits of clothes when they come of age. The boy ditto and implements of his trade, viz: That of tailor.

Will of Robert Beavers, decd. produced and proved by William Headen and Solomon Strickland, ordered to be recorded.

Petition of Joseph Ratchford that Jacob Summerford in his lifetime made bond for title to a certain tract of land in the State of Georgia which was coming to the said Jacob for his services in said State under Col. C l a r k, that good titles be given by Jacob's adm. Granted. Test. Ethelred Wood, B. Harris, James Hendrix.

COURT OF ORDINARY April 22, 1805.

Abraham Scott, one of the adm. of Jas. Knox, decd. makes returns.

Ditto Garrett W. Parks, on the est. of Robert Park, dec.

Ditto Bozeman Adair, adm. of John Nelson, decd.

COURT OF ORDINARY July 22, 1805.

William Otwell prays for a n d ontains letters of adm.on estate of John Baggett deceased.

Ordered that Abraham Scott & Ann Knox be appointed guardians of Polly Knox and David Luckie Knox, orphans of James Knox deceased.

Joseph Hambrick came into court and stated that his brother Burwell Hambrick a minor, has property to the amount of $160.00 in the h a n d s of the adm. of their decd. father, Thomas Hambrick, and t h a t Joseph be appointed guardian to said Burwell. Granted.

Bozeman A d a i r, Esq. states to the Court that Catey Ramsey, a citizen of Jackson County, has had several illegitimate children. Amongst t h e m one is said to be the child of Robert Adair, decd. and acknowledged by him in his lifetime. The said Bozeman being desirious that this child, James Ramsey, be educated, etc. as requested by his brother in his lifetime. Asked to be appointed guardian. Granted.

ORDINARY COURT. Oct. 28, 1805.

Richard Anderson prays for and obtains letters of adm. on the estate of Nathan Anderson, late of this county, decd.

Ann Stubblefield, an orphan child with no estate, bound to Samuel Barnett until 18 years of age.

Lewis Deal appointed guardian of the orphans of William Deal, decd. To-wit: Eleanor, Nancy a n d Stephen Deal. Bond $2,000.

Joshua, Robert and William Berry, orphans of John Berry,decd. Their father's estate not sufficient for their support. Joshua & William bound to William Cates until t h e.y are 21. Joshua being seven years old last Sept. 28th. William, two years old, 16th, of June last. Robert Berry bound to Joshua Betts. Robert being seven years old Feb. 20, next.

COURT OF ORDINARY Feb. 6, 1806.

William Potts, Security f o r Abraham Scott and Ann Knox, as guardian of Polly and David Luckie Knox, orphans of James Knox, decd. said Ann Knox having since intermariied with Isaac Cowan and Isaac appointed guardian with Thomas Ewing as Security.

EARLIER COURT RECORDS

January 2nd, 1797. Thomas Good to John Richard? Hart, both of Oglethorpe County; land on Big Shoal Creek. Test. Jas. Thomas, J.P.

Jan. 2, 1798. Ambrose Holliday of Warren County to J o h n McFalls of Jackson County, land in Oglethorpe County, when surveyed, in Wilkes County. Test. Barnett Brewett? Arthur Forte, J.P.

Nov. 6, 1796. John Bender to Ignatius Few, both of Richmond County, land on Middle Fork of Oconee River in Franklin County, originally granted to Bender 1797? Test. H. Drane and James Stallings.

Mar. 12th, 1797. John Cobb to Micajah B e n g e and William Hopkins of Jackson County, land on Barber's Creek and Oconee River. Test. John Morings. Elias Mobley.

May 10th, 1788. John Bender to Ignatius F e w, both of Richmond County, land on Middle Fork, Oconee River, Franklin Cty.

Sept. 4th, 1796. Jonothan Jackson Hays and wife, to S a m u e l Phillips, all of Franklin County, land in Franklin County when surveyed, Now Jackson County. Granted to J e n n y Phillips, now the wife of said Hays, Sept. 24th, 1788. Test. Moses McLure, Joseph Chandler, J.P.

Aug. 20, 1798. William Stokes, Dep. T. C., of Jackson County, to Brantley Sharks of Jackson County, 100 acres on Big Shoal C r e e k, granted in the name of James Stewart, but given in by Jesse Sparks as Trustee for the widow and orphans of Matthew Sparks. (May be Sharks). Test: Randall Traylor, J.P.

Mar. 7th, 1798. Joseph Scott and wife, Susannah, to Prosser Horton, 200 acres on Currie's Creek, part of a tract of 862 1/2 acres originally granted to Thomas Carson. Test. Ann Scott, Jos. M. McCutchen

Nov. 17, 1797. Josiah Woods of Franklin County to Thomas Hill of Oglethorpe Cty. land on Barber's Creek. Test. Theopolius Hill, Abram Hill and Wm. Johnson, J.P.

William P a y t o n of Elbert County to Alex Morrison of Jackson County, land on Sandy Creek. Test. W. Carter, Matthew Knight.

Sept. 19, 1797. William Sharks to Richard Nall 320 acres, part of tract granted to Wm. Sharks in 1791. Test. Champion T. Traylor, Martin Nall & Randall Traylor.

Jan. 12, 1798. Thomas Duke, Sr. of Oglethorpe County a n d Matthew Stone of Jackson County to John Barnett of Jackson County, originally granted to John Freeman Mar. 15th, 1787. Test. William Duke & William Strong.

WILL. Stephen Borders. s/ Jan. 9, 1839. p/ Mar. 4, 1839. Mother and Father, names not given. Brothers Enoch H., Michael and J o h n. Sisters: Ann, Lucinda, Matilda, Polly and Malinda. Nephew Stephen Thornton. Test. James Hargrove. Eli Shankle, Hardy Minish.

WILL. Tandy Key. s/ June 1836. p/ Dec. 17th, 1838. Wife, not named and daughter Harriett Phelps and her children. Children of daughter M a r y Mitchell, decd. Daughter Virginia Appleby and her children. Daughter Caroline Clark a n d her children. Daughter Susannah Wilkerson and her children. Sons: James C., George W. Daughter Martha Ann Moreland and her children. Daughter Melissa a n d Lem_? and her children. Daughter Elizabeth _? and her children. Son Madison Troup. Son Tandy. Son Thomas Jefferson. All younger children to have an education out of the estate. Son James C., John Appleby and John Wilson Executors. Test. Elisha Winn H. Webb. (Proven in Russell County Ala. Dec. 1838).

WILL. John G. Henderson. s/ May 10th, 1839. p/ June 1, 1839. (Planter). Plantation to youngest son, James D. Henderson, with son Andrew H. Henderson, both to take care of well-beloved wife, Margaret Henderson. Daughter Rebecca Henderson. Other children, names not given. Sons Andrew H. and James D., Exrs. Test: Nathaniel Harbin, James H. Daniel, Perry Bowen.

WILL. Joseph Harris. s/ July 25, 1832. p/ Sept. 2nd, 1839. Son Walton Harris. Wife, Elizabeth, if she marries, property to be sold and divided amongst the lawful heirs. Test: George W. Vinson, Moses Vinson and M.A.B rooks, J.P.

WILL. Harriett Willingham. s/ Feb.1839. p/ Sept. 2, 1839. My beloved mother, name not given. To sister Elizabeth Willingham, her share of her mother's dowry of the land on which she lives. Test. Solomon Chandler. Early M. Chandler, Lemuel Swan.

WILL... James Smith, s/ Aug. 25th, 1839. p/ Nov. 4, 1839. Sons: Charles, Alford, James M. Smith. Daughters: Dianna, Martha and Elizabeth. Ephraim Jackson and two sons Alford and James M. Smith, Exrs. Test: John Moon, Thomas Johnson. M. A. Brooks, J.P.

WILL. Alexander Morrison. s/ Feb. 6, p/ Jan. 6th, 1840. Wife Mary Ann. Three sons: Alexander R., Horatio M., and Cicero. Thomas J., Edward, Alexander R. Wife Mary Ann, three sons, Alexander R. Horatio M. and Cicero. Thomas J., Edwin R. and Alfred W. Morrison. Daughters Elizabeth Ann Dougherty, Harriett C. Hood, Elizabeth B. Bacon, Sons Thomas J. and Alfred Morrison and son-in-law Chas. Dougherty, Exrs. Test. Charles Dougherty Sr., Jas. Dougherty and Giles Mitchell.

WILL. Ann Nicholson. s/ Dec. 25, 1839. p/ Jan. 5th, 1840. Nieces: Jane and Mary Ann Patrick. The balance to be divided with my brothers and sisters -not named. Robert C. Patrick, Exr. Test: Harry A. Archer and John Patrick.

WILL. Tabitha Chandler. s/ May 25th, 1839. p/ July 6, 1840. Caroline House, Charlottey Adeline House, Elizabeth Tabaitha House, Frances Merretts House, Ann House, Elizabeth Chandler, Bailey's wife If Merrett Chandler and Miss Witt should marry, $1.50 each and no more. The other furniture to be divided between Samuel Bailey House, John Jeremiah Thomas House and Felix Littleberry House; Jane and Amanda House. Test: James, Charity, Mary Shields.

WILL. John King Sr. s/ Dec. 27, 1839. p/ July 7, 1840. Son John. Son David H., Son James King. Son-in-law Charles Miller. Son-in-law Robert Espey. Son-in-law Charles DuPree, Lot No. 317, Telfair Cty granted to Charles Miller and deeded by him to me. Daughter C. Elizabeth Espey, wife of Robert. Wife mentioned but not named. Five children of my daughter Jane Miller, decd. Eleven children of my daughter, Petty Espey. To Mary Ahn Briant, $25.00. (relationship not given). Robert Espy, John King Jr., David H. King, Exrs. Test. M.T. Wilhite, Sterling May. Joel C. Neal.

WILL. Ansel Cunningham. s/ Aug. 22nd 1840. p/ Sept. 7th, 1840. Old and infirm, wife Mary. Grandson: Middleton Cox. To James Montgomery $500.00. Property to be equally divided between Thomas Barnes, Drury Cunningham, James Montgomery, Ansel C., John H., William J. Cunningham and James Cunningham, orphans. Thomas Barnes, James Montgomery, John H. and William J. Cunningham, Exrs. Test. Richard Wilbanks, Richard Williamson and Wm. M. Winters.

WILL. Elizabeth Heard. s/ Apr. 5, 1839. p/ Sept. 1840. To son Charles M. and Daniel C. Heard, $1.00. To son-in-law James Tabbs, $1.00. Daughter Mary Heard, grand-son, John Armstrong Head, son of Charles M. Heard. Granddaughter Isabelle Emeline Tabbs, under age. Grandson Richard Heard Cheely, son of Mary Heard, Mary Heard, residuary legatee. Lewis and Wm. Southward Tabbs, sons of James Tabbs, Asa Varnum, Exr. Test. John Glenn, Roderick Matthews. Amanda C. Chesly.
ABOVE. Southard correct. May also be Cheely instead Chesly or visa versa.

WILL. William Beavers. s/ Aug. 10, 1840 p/ Nov. 2, 1840. Wife Susannah, "my children when they come of age" Wife Susannah and James Tolbert, Exrs. Test. Abner Willis, Archibald and Boler Moon.

WILL. Isaac Titsmouth. s/ Mar. 1, 1839. p/ Nov. 1840. Grandson Neriah? Lewis Bennett, Granddaughter Patsy Paul Bennett and heirs of my daughter Elizabeth Bennett, decd. Daughter Nancy Barron and son in-law Samuel Barron, her husband. Grand son Thomas Nix, the only surviving child of my daughter Rebecca Nix, decd. Grandchildren: Amanda, Elizabeth, Isaac N., Thomas, Marshall, William and Calvin Barron, being the children of my deceased daughter, Sally Barron, to them severally as they come of age, the homeplace of 400 acres to be appr. and neighbor Morrison to have refusal of it. Presly Hardy and Thomas Morrison appointed guardians of my good old faithful Negro Marcher? She is to have her freedom and $100.00. Friend Hardy Strickland and Wm. M. Gathright, Exrs. Test. Preston Hardy, Edward Wills and A.W. Morrison.

WILL. James Barr. s/ 1835. p/ Mar. 1841. Wife Mary, life estate. Plantation to go to son, James Henson? Barr. The balance to be sold and equally divided among all my children, James, Mary Barr, James Henson? Barr and Boley Wilson, Exrs. Test. James Montgomery, John Cunningham and Samuel Hay.

WILL. Adah Petty. s/ July 2, 1839. P/ Mar. 1st, 1841. Father Alex Petty, life estate in home. To be divided among Celina and Letty Ann Dixon, and the rest of William Dixon's children and Berrilaby N. Seats, if she ever has any children. Father Alex Petty, Exr. Test. Levi Benton, Mary A. Ross, William Dixon.

WILL. Mary Cochran. s/ Nov. 24, 1836. p/ Nov. 30th, 1841. To John Wallace Sr. $65.00 and $45.00 to be paid to Jeremiah Reeves for the use of Walmont? church. The residue to be equally divided between my three daughters, viz: Judith Winn, Ann Key, Jane Thurmond & my grand daughter Mary Ann DeLaprierre; and my son Simeon Wilkes. Harrison Thurmond, Elisha Winn and Angel LaPrierre; Executors. Test. Peter E. McMillan, Hilliard J Randolph, Jacob Braselton.

WILL. John King. s/ Jan. 1st, 1842. p/ Mar. 7th, 1842. Wife Elizabeth (Johnson) half of estate, real and personal, heirs of my step-son Christopher Kimble, one-fourth. Heirs of my step-son Patrick, one fourth & $100.00 to Elizabeth Minish, an invalid of the county. Wife Elizabeth and friend Thomas J. Davis, Exrs. Test. Giles Mitchell, James Garvin, Andrew M. Park.

WILL. Phillip Ryan. s/ Apr. 29, 1836. p/ May 3rd, 1842. Wife Rachael, home and Negro as long as she is a widow or remaining in the home. If she marries or moves, everything to go to Westly Nance of Clarke County. Test. George Dent. S. Thomas, Jr. Ephraim Jackson.

WILL. Thomas Black. s/ Jan. 1839. p/ Jan. 4, 1842. Wife Margaret, life estate to be divided between my seven children: viz: Samuel, Cynthia, Amelia, Hugh (married Emily Howard), Augustine, Virginia and Caroline. Sons: Samuel J. and Augustine, Exrs. Test. Joseph David, James Appleby, John Wallace.

WILL. John Stovall. s/ Sept. 22, 1842. p/ Jan. 1843. Wife Mariah, life estate. Children: Jeptha A., Emily, Harriett, William W., Martha, Margaret, Mary, Mariah and Julian, under age. Wife Mariah, William W. Stovall, James M. Smith, Exrs. Test: M. T. Wilhite, Robert White, S. R Street.

WILL. Jane Jones. s/ May 2nd, 1841. p/ July 10, 1843. To friend and son-in-law, William Hamilton, a slave. Son James Jones, Exr. Test. Russell Barker, Green W. Smith and Reddick Betts.

EARLY COURT RECORDS.

Dec. 11, 1792. George Hendley, Sheriff of Richmond County, to Jack and Robert Middleton of Washington County, land in Franklin County taken by a suit of Richard Wylly and Leonard Cecil? at a court in Wilkes County. Test. Wm. Robertson & D. Hunter, J.P.

May 9th, 1795. James R. Whitney, T.C. Franklin County, to John Cobb. Surveyed for Leonard Marbury, 1785 acres. Test. Samuel Gardner and Thomas Payne.

Nov. 26th, 1798. John Webster to Moses Webster Sr. bill of sale for cattle, appraised by Jacob Myers and Jas. Taylor.. Test. John McConnell Jr.

Jan. 4, 1799. Francis Gideon and wife, Elizabeth, of Wilkes County, to Jacob Littleton of Warren County, $60 for 575 acres. Test. Lewis Irvin & A. Bailey.

Jan. 16, 1799. Grant Taylor to Matthew Barber, a certain tract of land for $10. Test. J. Stewart.

Jan. 24, 1799. Jacob Littleton and wife Milly of Warren County to Elijah Pope of N.C., formerly of Oglethorpe County Ga. for land on Sandy Creek. Test. Paul Patrick, J.P.

Apr. 6, 1790. John Peter Wagnon to John Cobbs, 9487 1/2 acres granted to said Wagnon in 1786. 3,000 acres on Barber's Creek, McMills and Bears Creek; 287 1/2 acres granted to Littleberry Williams on Hurricane Shoals. Test. John Poythress, William Howell.

Feb. 6th, 1799. Charles Davidson and wife, Judith, to Robert Gilham, land in Cumberland County Va. on Cannon's Creek, adjacent to Robert Carrington and Philemon Davidson. Test. William Strong, J.P.

Feb. 16th, 1799. John Cobb to Benjamin Easley. Test. George Taylor. R. Easley.

Nov. 5th, 1797. Cordy Pate to William Williamson, both of Oglethorpe County, land on Walnut Creek, part of a survey to George McFall 1792. Test. John, Jacob and Abram Lindsey.

Feb. 24th, 1799. William Strong Jr. to Jesse Flippant? 140 acres on Big Creek part of original grant to Thomas Walton in 1785. Test. William Strong, J.P.

May 9th, 1795. James R. Whitney, T.C. for Franklin County, to John Cobb, 287 1/2 acres surveyed for William Love Oct. 1784. Test. George Taylor. Geo. Hemming.

Dec. 5th, 1794. James R. Whitney, T.C. for Franklin County, to John C o b b and J o h n Benning, 1150 acres originally granted to Leonard Marbury in 1785. Test Joseph Benning and Geo. Hemming.

Dec. 5th, 1794. Same parties, 287 1/2 acres, originally granted to Abraham Bradley in 1784. Test. same.

Dec. 5th, 1794. James R. Whitney, T.C. for Franklin County, same parties, 230 acres surveyed for James Russell in 1780 Test. Joseph Benning and Geo. Hemming.

Dec. 5th, 1794. James R. Whitney, T.C. for Franklin County, land surveyed for George Brewer in 1784. Test. Joseph Benning and Geo Hemming.

Dec. 5th, 1794. James R. Whitney, T.C. for Franklin County, land surveyed for Edward McGary in 1790. Test. same

Same date as above. Land surveyed for John Lynch in 1784.

Same date as above. Land surveyed for Horatio Marbury in 1785.

Nov. 24th, 1798. David Hillhouse of Wilkes Cty. to Roderick Easley of Jackson County for various sums of money advanced, labor, etc. grants 1/2 part of Addulum?Furnace? on south of Broad River Test. P. Jack. G. Gaines.

Jan. 24th, 1799. James B. Dharpe (Dr. Boyd) of Burke County, to Roderick Easley of Jackson County, 690 acres on Oconee River, originally granted to James B. Sharpe in 1790. Test W.S. Smith, Robt. Jackson.

Jan. 16, 1796. Ezekiel Offutt of Warren County to Joseph McCutchen of Jackson County, 287 1/2 acres on North fork of Oconee River. Originally granted to Malachi Culpepper in 1793. From him to said Offutt. Test. Abram Scott, James Ewing, Thomas Kirkpatrick, J.P.

Jan. 1st, 1799. Charles Harvy, Sr. of Jefferson County, to Roderick Easley, 287 1/2 acres on Sandy Creek. Test. John Cobb and E. Hargrove.

Nov. 5th, 1794. James R. Whitney, of Franklin County, s a m e as above, land surveyed in the name of John Rossau 1787 Test. Jos. Benning. Geo. Hemming.

Mar. 13th, 1799. Alexa Patrick to Millican Patrick, cattle, household goods, etc. for $500. Test. Luke Patrick, Paul Patrick, J.P.

Mar. 15, 1799. John Cobb of Jefferson County, to Roderick Easley of Jackson County. Test. B. Easley, Robert Jackson.

Mar. 14, 1798. Samuel Knox to Susannah Cox of Wilkes County, 100 acres on Rocky Creek formerly Franklin County, now Jackson County, part of a double bounty surveyed for John Partin and conveyed by William Nichols to said Know. Test. Chas. Dougherty and J. George.

Feb. 2nd, 1799. Joseph East and wife Milly to Charles Henderson of Oglethorpe County, 287 1/2 acres on Sandy Creek. Test. James Pittman, J.P.

Mar. 14, 1798. Samuel Knox to Susannah Cox of Wilkes County, 575 acres granted to Daniel Butler in 1785. Conveyed by him to said Knox on Big Creek, Franklin County, now Jackson County. Test. Chas. Dougherty and J. George.

Feb. 3rd, 1799. Luke Tatum of S.C. to Evans Long of Wilkes County, 300 acres on Sandy Creek. Test. Matthew Tolbert, Hillory Hendrix.

May 10, 1798. Basil Jones of Columbia County to Arthur Talbot of Jackson Cty. 250 acres of land on north fork, Oconee River, granted to Jones in 1798. Test. James McMillen, Absolom Rainey.

Feb. 10, 1799. John Langdon of Wilkes County, to Talbot Arthur of Jackson Cty. 287 1/2 acres on Big Shoal Creek. Test. Absolom Rainey, J.P.

Dec. 6, 1797. John Thurmond to Charles Thurmond, both of Wilkes County, land on Oconee River in Jackson County. Test. Wm. Thurmond. Absolom Thurmond.

July 13, 1798. Samuel Gamble and wife, Jane, of Abbeville, S. C. to John Gamble of Lincoln County Georgia 287 1/2 acres in Jackson County Georgia, formerly in Franklin County, north fork of Oconee River, granted to John Hubbard June 18, 1786 and conveyed by deed to Samuel Gamble and his wife. Test. Robert Gamble Richard Camp and Elihu Keith.

Dec. 29th, 1798. Jeffry Early of Oglethorpe County, to John Strong Sr. of Jackson County, land in Franklin County, when surveyed, now in Jackson County, at head of Big Creek, granted to Henry Karr on bounty Jan. 15th, 1785, part of it granted to heirs of Greenberry Chaney Jan. 19th, 1785. Test. Wm. Strong, James Price, John Moss.

Apr. 4, 1799. Thomas Brown of Jackson County, gives power of attorney to James Henderson of Pittsylvania County Va. to sell a tract of land in said county, willed to 'my wife', Betty Ann, in part by her father, James Buckley, of said county, decd. Test. Absolom Rainey, J.P. Paul Patrick, J.P.

Mar. 2, 1799. William Strong, Esq. to John Strong Sr., land on Big Creek, part of original survey to Thomas Walton in 1785. Test. Wm. M. Stokes, J.P.

Nov. term of Court 1802. B. Harris, A. Rainey, J. Pittman, Esq. Petition of Jas Akin, praying that Peter Akin, an orphan be bound to a suitable person. It is or- that upon the Clerk receiving a CERTIFI- CATE from the Clerk of Oglethorpe County that Peter be bound, etc. and give Micajach Williamson an indenture of said Peter, etc. M.M. Nall Clerk.

Charles Dougherty appointed guardian to Charles Smith, Elizabeth Smith and Leucy Smith.

Martha Rogers, widow of Thomas Rogers, appointed guardian of David Rogers, Thomas Stanfer Rogers, Mary Rogers and John Henderson Rogers, heirs of said deceased. Upon the petition of Obedience Rogers, one of the heirs and representatives of John Rogers, Esquire, decd. Prior Thornton appointed her guardian.

Aug. 4th, 1802. Swan Harden ordered to turn over the property of Austin N. and William Blackburn to Isaac Hill. Recorded Nov. Court 1802.

COURT OF ORDINARY Feb. 3rd, 1802. Present: James Pittman, William Foster, James Hendricks, Esquires.

Samuel Henderson granted letters of administration on the estate of Richard Moore, deceased.

David Kinsey granted letters of adm. in estate of James Kinsey, decd.

Ordered that adms. and Exrs. and guardians, bound to make annual returns to this county, who have fallen in to Clarke upon producing a receipt from Clerk of Clarke County, be excused, ditto for this county.

ORDINARY'S COURT Mar. 8, 1802. Present their honors: Buckner Harris, James Pittman, William Foster, James Hendricks.

Petition of John Thurmond, endorsee of Richard Thurmond by Walton Harris, atty. that the heirs of Bartholomew Zachary, of Wilkes County, make titles to land on Oconee River in the Continental Reserve near the Apalashee in Greene County, 690 acres adjacent to Andrew Baxter, surveyed for said Baxter Mar. 11th, 1786, sold to Curtis Welbourn by him to said Thurmond. Test. Archer Land. William Thurmond.

Petition of Joseph Ratchford by Walton Harris, atty. that Richard Moore of this county, April 9, 1784, bound himself in the sum of 100 lbs. to be paid to Joseph Ratchford by making good titles to a certain tract of 287 1/2 acres due to him for his services in the State, as soon as said Ratchford shall get the grant out of the office. Ordered that titles be made by the adm. of said Richard Moore, decd. In this indenture, Richard Moore calls himself of Camden Dist. S. C. and conveys this land which was granted him for services in Ga. Test Jos Henderson.

Petition of Daniel and Martha Johnson, formerly Martha Rogers, relict and widow Thomas Rogers, decd. late of this county, stating that the said decd. left four children: David Rogers, Thomas Stanfer Rogers, Mary Rogers and John Henderson Rogers, asking for thier guardianship. Granted.

Ordered that Peleg Rogers, adm. of the estate of Thomas Rogers, decd. render to the court a perfect inventory of personal property in his hands since the decease of said Thomas Rogers.

Jan. 1798. Estate of Benjamin Watson, decd., debtor to Joseph Humpries for advertising and hiring four Negroes, to-wit: Jude, Lucy, Charles and Celia, which Negroes were found by said Humphries in the estate of Augustine Blackburn, dec. which were sold by the Sheriff to satisfy a mortgage in favor of estate of Blackburn. Statement April 1799 includes clothes for these slaves and $12 advanced to Daniel Pinkston for taking care of Sarah Watson, a woman of insanity, widow of said Benjamin Watson, from the 10th, day of Dec. to sometime in the following Spring. Edward Adams, Clerk.

ORDINARY'S COURT, first Monday July 1802. Present, their Honors: David Dixon James Hendricks, William Foster, James Pittman, Esquires. Petition of Frances Neal asking that she be dismissed as admx. of Joseph Neal, deceased, and that the other two adms., to-wit: John and Julian Neal, be appointed. Granted.

Petition of James Moore that to be appointed adm. of the estate of Michael Moore, decd. advertisement having been made. Granted.

Esther McCord applied for and granted letters of adm. on the estate of Abraham McCord, Decd.

John Spears and Joseph Cowling, Exrs. of the estate of Benjamin Cowling, decd. make retures for 1801.

Isaac Hill asks to be and is released as Exr. of the will of Isaac Hill, dec. Having found the said decd. was under age at the time of his death, and had never had his property in his own hands.

On motion of William Harris, Obediah Light was ordered to pay money for the support of a bastard child.

Peleg Rogers, adm. of the estate of Thomas Rogers, decd. ordered to make returns of said estate at the next Court. And that Daniel Johnston, in right of his wife, formerly the wife of said Thomas Rogers, decd. also attend.

ORDINARY'S COURT, Tues. Aug. 2, 1802. Present: Buckner Harris, James Hendricks David Dixon, James Pittman, Esquires. Ordered that the Court of Ordinary sit quarter yearly the fourth Mondays in Oct., Jan., April and July.

Obediah Light having failed to comply with the law, held to bail. Walton Harris Esquire, presecuting attorney.

Bozeman Adair, adm.. of the estate of John Nelson, decd., makes returns.

Sarah Briants, admx. estate of Benjamin Briants, made returns for 1801.

Charles Dougherty, adm. of the estate of Francis L o y a l? decd. made returns. Also a return in right of his wife, Rebecca Dougherty, extx. of the estate of William Puryear, decd.

WILL. Lewis Hiner. s/ Feb. 21, 1830. p/ May 3, 1830. Wife Nancy. C hildren: Abraham, Edwin a n d Nancy Hiner, under age. John and Jacob Hiner, land already given. Mary Milsaps, a tract of land in Clarke County on which Hiram Milsaps lives, to be given to his son John Milsaps. John and Nancy Hiner, Extrs. Test. Marvel Milsaps, Josiah Wallis and James Stuart.

WILL. William Reynolds. s/ Aug. 4, 1829. p/ July 5th, 1830. Wife Ann. "Heirs" Son John Reynolds. Patsy King, Patsy Pendengrass, Sarah West; Rhoda Patterson a n d Frances Gilham a n d Amanda Caroline Reynolds, daughter of Travis Reynolds, under age. Test. James R. McCleskey, Jesse Pate. [The above should be ELIZABETH KING]

WILL. John Winters. s/ Sept. 1829. p/ July 5, 1830. Wife Charity(Patton). Slaves left to me by Samuel Patton, until he becomes 21 years old, some in possession of Stephen Dale, 490 acres Lot No. 87, 15th, District Irwin County, not yet granted a n d the property coming to her from her father's estate, she being at liberty to give her ch ldren such property as she pleases as they advance in years. Wife Charity a n d her son William K. Winters, Extrs. Test G.W.Albert and Nancy Winters.

WILL. Elizabeth Brazeal. s/ June 16th, 1830. p/ Sept. 6, 1830. To Charles Dougherty, Jr. Lot No. 180, 3rd, District Lee County, draw in her name in the last lottery, said Charles sole Executor. Test. Edward Adams, Dr., Chas. Dougherty, Sr. and Elizabeth Dougherty.

WILL. William Bennett(Planter). s/ July 25th, 1822. p/ Not shown. Wife Rachael. Son Hezekiah. Daughter Sarah Hardy. Son Armstead. Daughter Judy Hardy. Daughter Polly Perry, $20.00. To daughter Patsy Bennett $20.00. To son, Thomas Bennett, (wife Nancy Bass) a cow and calf. To son Asa Bennett, a horse, etc. Son William, and Bartley Bennett. Wife and sons William and Thomas, extrs. Test. Absolom, Abraham and Jonothan Crisler.

WILL. George Wilson Sr. s/ May 1, 1823. No d a t e of probation. To be buried by wife. To son Benjamin, son-in-law James Haggard and wife. Son Robert. Son George W. Son-in-law John Casey a n d wife. Son John. Son Thomas. Son-in-law Moses Vinson a n d wife. Son James, .25 cents each. Grandson Geor ge Vinson, his desk. Son Wm. all l a n d, bed, etc. to Martha Vinson. Test. Jesse Harris, Magmus Brooks.

WILL. Micajah Williamson, Attorney-at-law. s/ Sept. 1803. No date of probation To brother, William Williamson, slaves. Eo w i f e Polly, rest of the estate and sole Extx. Test. D. Criswell, J.M.Carrol and Jett Thomas.

WILL. John Justus. s/ Nov. 9, 1829. p/ Jan. 3, 1831. Sons: David, Henry, Allen, a n d Stephen Justus. Daughters Kezziah - Patsy McCutcheon and Dolly Blalock. Grandchildren: Elvira Justus, eldest daughter of my son Stephen. James Johnson Justus. Bess Gillium? Justus a n d Thirsda Justus, heirs of my son William Justus, decd. Son-in-law Aaron Combs and H e n r y Justus, Exrs. Test. Edward Pharr, David Bradford, George Bradford.

WILL. John Martin. s/ Apr. 16th, 1830. p/ Feb. 8, 1831. Wife Mary, home plantation and all the appurtenances for the support of my daughters, Nancy and Ruthy during their virginity, and a home for my younger sons until they become of age Sons William, Levi, Elisha, John, Elijah, Malachi & Simeon Martin. Daughter Betsy Hunter. Wife Mary, sole Extrx. Test. John J. McCulloch, James Shields.

WILL. Joseph Harrison. s/Feb. 9, 1831. p/ Mar. 7, 1831. Son Colmore. Granddaughter Malinda Cavin. Grandson William Cavin. Children of Meeky Holland(daughter) wife of John Holland. Sons: Josephus, Overton, Jason and Tilman Harrison. Ichabod Manson?child of Rebecca Kinningham, acknowledged by my son, Hezekiah, to be his child. Money left to build a stone wall to include a 14 foot square to include the grave of my daughter Susan and her child. Son Tilman Harrison, Exr. Test. Jacob Callahan, William McMullen.

WILL. Isaac Boring. s/ Sept. 4, 1829. p/ June 7, 1831. Wife Phoebe Boring, all the land and plantation on which I now live & appurtenances and, Negroes: Moses Jane, Esther, Lewis, Mariah, Reuben, Willis, Caroline, Clary, Mary and Polly.
  Children: John, Robert, Isaac Boring. Elizabeth Lyle, Phoebe Johnson, Susannah Tait. Grandchildren: Asenith, Sarah, Elizabeth, Joseph and Penelope Adams. Delilah Tait, Mary Tait, grandchildren by my daughter, Asenith Wafer, decd. Thomas and James Jackson Wafer, under age. Mentioned lands in Lee County, Gwinnett County and Jackson County where David Thomas formerly lived, adjacent to Waid Slaton. Wife Phoebe, John and Isaac Boring, exrs. Test. W. Pentecost, Edmund Honeycutt, Richard Pentecost.

WILL. Russell Jones of Franklin County s/ Dec. 21, 1827. p/ Mar. 3, 1828. Wife, Sarah. Slaves returned as per marriage contract. Son Russell Jones. Son-in-law Allen Daniel and Polly Daniel.(WIFE). Her children except William Daniel, deducting from Oliver Powell's proportion $240 Heirs of my son Dudley Jones, decd. Illegitimate daughter of my granddaughter Nancy Hooper, son-in-law Benjamin Cleveland.
  Six grandchildren of daughter, Amelia Allen, decd. Son-in-law Asa Allen, five dollars. Son-in-law Charles Sorrels. Sons: Lewis, Thomas, William and James Jones. Wife and son Russell, exrs. Test. Gray Allen, Hugh A. Thompson, Russell F. Jones.

WILL. Chandler Flagg. Nun-cupative. Dec. 13/4th, 1830. Debts to be paid out of the proceeds of his shop and Zenas Hubbard to have the rest. Present: Francis Hopson, Thomas Adams, Sarah Bacon and Zenas Hubbard, the legatee.

WILL. Robert Venable. p/ Jan. 3, 1832. Wife Isabella. Life estate in everything including a farm whereon Henry Mann now lives and land near Gainesville in Hall County. (children under age, names not given). Wife Isabella and James M. Cunningham, exrs. Test. Jesse Murphy, Madison Montgomery, Thomas Shockley.

WILL. William Shaw. s/ June 3rd, 1831. p/ Nov. 7, 1831. Wife Susannah(George). Daughter Permelia. Daughters: Elizabeth Landers, Mary Rasbury, Nancy Summers, Jincey Glawson. Wife Susannah, William, Nathan, James and Bryan Shaw, Exrs. Test. David J. Lyle, Richard Pentecost, Austin Fulcher.

WILL. John Gilbert. s/ Nov. 5th, 1831. p/ July 2, 1832. Negroes to be hired out until a sufficient sum for transporting them to another State in the U. S. where they will be free by the laws of the country. Friend Wood Hinton, Exr. Test. Little B. Slaton, John S. Shields. John G. Howse.

WILL. Rachael Wallace. s/ July 13th, 1832. p/ Aug. 7, 1832. Three daughters: Nancy Spence, Kizziah Wattrour and Rachael Tredwell. Marvel Milsaps, Exr. Test. Marvel Milsaps, Jacob Hiner, Abram Hiner.

WILL. John M. Crawford. s/ Sept. 1st, 1831. p/ May 7th, 1832. Wife Polly, land in 6th, District of Houston County. Her three children: Chas. Grisham Crawford, Ebenezer Sanford Crawford and James Benjamin Crawford. My first children: Thos. Crawford and Sarah Ann Crawford. Joseph Maddox and John Creighton, Exrs. Test. John McDonald, William Dixon, John G. Pittman.

WILL. Charles McKinney, Jr. s/ May 31, 1832. p/ Aug. 6, 1832. (record shows he married Nancy Hogan in 1828). To my sister Rachael Webb, $100.00, for her attention to me and taking care of my eldest daughter, since the death of its mother, $100.00. To Miss Frances Hogan, ditto for youngest daughter. The rest to be divided between my two daughters, Polly Ann and Milda? Ann McKinney, when they become of lawful age. Exrs. Elijah Clowe? Nathaniel Shotwell. Jesse S. Shotwell, James Sisson.

WILL. Joseph Ratchford, Sr. s/ May 11, 1832. p/ Oct. 1st, 1832. Daughter Polly and her heirs, if she has any. Son Jos. property in trust of son, Ezekiel. Son James. Son Robert, nine rods square reserved at the grave yard for family burial ground. (Wife mentioned but not named.) Two sons Robert and Ezekiel, Exrs. Test. Allen Matthews, Sr. Nancy C. Matthews and Mary Matthews.

WILL. Thomas R.G. Adams. s/ Oct. 24th, 1832. p/ Noc. 2nd, 1832. Wife Caroline. [Watts] and children, names not given. Wife Caroline and William Appleby, Exrs. Test. G. F. Adams, J.M. Cunningham, John Johnston.

WILL. David Justus. p/ Jan. 13, 1833. Wife Sarah. Estate to be disposed of by her and my son, William, for the support and education of my little children. Test. Edward Pharr, Hezekiah W. Pharr, Benjamin Scroggins.

WILL. Travis Nixon. s/ May 9, 1833. p/ July 10th, 1833. Wife Susannah, "land in Lee County and in the Gold Region, which I have lately drawn in the gold lottery". Sons: Henry, William and John. Daughters Lydia Strawbridge, Elizabeth Archer, Sarah Collier and Rebecca Robinson. Son-in-law Isaac Knox. Dianna Allen, formerly wife of my son Tapley Nixon. Wife Susannah and Asa Varnum, Exrs. Test Walter Mitchell, James Peach, William Bell.

WILL. Absolom Wofford. s/Oct. 18, 1832 No date of probation. Granddaughter Elizabeth Wofford, grandson John Wofford. Daughter Hannah Wallace, John Wallace Exr. Test John Clark, Mary Wallace.

WILL. Leonidas Few. s/ May 10th, 1833. p/ July 1st, 1833. Wife Martha (Lowry). "N. B. I gave to my father-in-law, Levi Lowry, bill of sale for said girl Susan, verbal consideration before Matthew McCullars and Alfred Few, that she was not to be taken from me." Sons: Camillas, LaFayette, Ignatius, William Simcon? and Leonidas Allen Few, and a child in esse. Wife Martha and son Camillas, Exrs. Land consist of 1760 acres in Franklin County 1000 acres in Jackson County on Currie's Creek, the homeplace. Test. H. Hemphill, Levi A.R.Lowry.

WILL. Charles McKinney. p/Mar. 3, 1834 "Far advanced in age". Wife Elizabeth, Daughter Rachael Webb. Horatio Webb, Willis Webb, Polly Lyle, Alcy Hampton, Wilborn Webb. R. D. Johnson and each of his children by my daughter Milda. Daughter Betsy Hearn. Sons William & Saml. Sarah Hampton, James Hampton and James Hargrove, exrs. Test. James Montgomery, Thomas Barnes, John G. Heard.

WILL. Thomas Phillips. s/ Sept. 20th, 1833. p/ May 5th, 1834. Wife Elizabeth. Five sons: Adam, John, Thomas, Henry and Levi. Sons Adam and Levi, Exrs. Test. Robert Smithwick, Robert Allen, Levi A. R. Lowry.

WILL. Rhoda Rogers. s/ May 29th, 1834. p/ June 2, 1834. Son James. Son Theopolius. Daughter Rhoda Rouden. Granddaughter. Rhoda Ann Kennedy. Daughter Mary B. Potts. All above these legacies to be divided among my children. Son James, Exr. Test. Claiborn Smith. M.T.Wilhite.

WILL. Andrew Cunningham. s/ Feb. 8th, 1834. p/ June 2, 1834. To brother Joseph T. Cunningham, land whereon I 'live, part to be reserved for the use of my mother Elizabeth Cunningham. To brother James T. Cunningham, land Lot No. 101, 10th, District Carroll County Ga. Nephews Edward and John Doss, Joseph Doss, James Doss, Hugh M. and Andrew Cunningham, niece Margaret Cunningham, other legatees George Doss, Green Doss, Garrett Doss, John R. Cunningham, Brother Joseph T. and Edward Story, Exrs. Test. Edward Story, James F. Story, John Richardson.

EARLY COURT RECORDS

Oct. 4th, 1796. Jonothan Jackson Hays, to Samuel Jackson Hays, both of Franklin County, land in Franklin County, originally surveyed for Jean Phillips and confirmed by grant Sept. 24th, 1788, to Jean now the wife of said Hays. $10 consideration land on Trail Creek. Test. Ezekiel Wells, Samuel Wells, Daniel Beall.

Oct. 27, 1795. John Shoddard and wife, Tabitha, of Abbeville S. C.,(County) to Isaac Middlebrooks Jr. land on Rocky Crk. originally granted to Barnabas Pace in 1784. Test. John Middleton and William Williams. Proved in Lincoln County by Wm. Williams.

Oct. 21st, 1795. James O'Brien of Montgomery County Maryland to James Perry of Prince George County Maryland, 230 acres. The same being in consideration of bounty lands assigned and granted and laid out for me in regard of my military services yielded as a soldier in the Georgia Regt. of soldiers in the soldiers against Great Britain. (in Franklin County). Friend Nathaniel Perry of Augusta, Richmond Cty. power of attorney to execute this deed. In places it written Perry - NOTE

Oct. 21st, 1795. Nathaniel Perre(Perry) of Augusta Ga. attorney for James O'Brien of Montgomery County Md. to Eli Perre, son of James Perre, then of Prince George Maryland, decd. who by his last will bequeathed above land to said son Eli, 230 acres on Ram's Branch, the Franklin Cty. now Jackson County, granted to said James O'Brien May 12, 1785 in consideration of military service performed by sd. O'Brien in S t a t e of Georgia. Test. William J. Hobby. Isaac Hubert, J.P.

Feb. 25, 1797. Moses Millican of Oglethorpe County to William Boyd of S. C. 200 acres on Oconee River, granted said Millican in 1796. Test. William McCree and John McRee.

Feb. 25, 1797. Moses Millican of Oglethorpe County to William Morrow of S. C., part of above tract. Test same as above.

Apr. 3, 1798. Charles Dougherty, Sheriff, to Russell Goodrich of Charleston, S. C., land, etc. of Thomas Herwood, sold for taxes in Franklin County and land on Currie's Creek, Jackson County Ga. Test. M. Williamson, R. Easley, J.P.

Sept. 19th, 1798. William Sharkis? to Randolph Traylor, 100, acres on Oconee River. Test. Champion F. Taylor. Martin Nall, Paul Patrick, Jr.

Mar. 31, 1798. Henry Anglin of Jackson County to Baptist Church on Trail Creek, for love and good will, land on Trail Creek near Oconee River by Cedar Shoal. Test. Paul Patric, J.P.

Aug. 16, 1797. William Nichols and wife Nancy, of Jackson County, to James Lockridge, land on Shoal Creek, where said Nichols now lives. Originally granted to John Partin Nov. 14, 1788. Test. John Armstrong, Arthur Patton, Benjamin Rice.

Jan. 24, 1798. John Barnett of Jackson County, to Robert Burke of Elbert County land on north Oconee, originally granted to James Stewart in 1785. Test. Samuel Pennington, Wm. Stone. Absolom Rainey.

Sept. 1797. Benjamin Vermillion and wife Tabitha, to Parks Chandler, land on the Oconee River, originally granted to said Vermillion July 5, 1786. Test. Jos. Humphries, J.P. Uriah Humphries.

MISCELLANEOUS RECORDS JACKSON COUNTY GEORGIA

Nov. 14, 1796. Joice Finch and Richard Copeland, Exrs. of the estate of Charles Finch, decd. of Oglethorpe County to Wm. Stephenson of Greene County, a planter, part of the t r a c t of a 1,000 acres on S h o a l Creek, granted to said Charles Finch Aug. 12,1789. Test. Thomas Rutledge and Burdett Finch.

Nov. 5th, 1796. Micajah Williamson of W i l k e s County, to Robert McAlpin of Greene County, land on Apalachie River, Jackson County. Test. Benjamin Taliaferro one of the Judges, John Griffin.

Aug. 25th, 1797. Joseph East and wife M i l l y, to Alexander Morrison, land on Sandy Creek, where said East now lives. Test. James Pittman, J.P.

Apr. 17, 1798. William Moore to George White, land on Sandy Creek, adjacent to widow Moore, originally granted to Wm. Moore. Test. Joseph East.

Jan. 9, 1797. Evan Long of Wilkes Cty. to Luke Tatum of S. C. 300 acres on Sandy Creek. Test. John Matthews. Geo. Matthews.

May 2, 1797? Thomas Johnson Beatty, of Georgetown, Montgomery County Md. to Wm. Deakins, ditto, for five shillings, two tracts of land, over 1,000 acres each in Franklin County, conveyed by Leonard Marbury to Beatty. Test. Thomas Cornovan?, Daniel Reintzell.

June 7th, 1798. James Gideon to J o h n Green, land on Currie Creek. Test. Joseph McCutchen, J.P.

May 26th, 1798. Thomas Kirkpatrick to Francis Kirkpatrick,124 acres on Currie's Creek. Test. Jos. McCutchen, J.P.

Dec. 24, 1796. Samuel Hemphill and wife Elizabeth of Greene County, to Radford Ellis of Oglethorpe County, the land on Opulacha River, Jackson County. Test. Wm. Ellis, George Verner, Matthew Varner.

Arthur Talbor a n d wife, Obedience, to William Jones,all of Jackson County, land on the south side of North Fork, Oconee River. T e s t. Joshua Stephens, Jeremiah Matthews.

Feb. 9, 1798. William Payton of Elbert County, to Alex Morrison of Jackson Cty. l a n d on Sandy Creek. Test. W. Carter, Matthew Knight.

Mar. 6th, 1798. John Barnett of Jackson County to John Patrick of Green County, land on north Oconee River, originally granted to Barnett in 1787. Test. [one name unreadable]. John Spiers.

Nov. 18th, 1797. Mial J. Barnett, to Jonothan Lee. Test. John Barnett. John Summers, William Strong.

Jan. 2, 1797. John Hart to Providence Sheppard, both of Jackson County, land on Shaol Creek. Test. Hugh Mars, J.P.

July 24th, 1798. Thomas Walton, Sr. of Franklin County, to William Strong, Sr. of Jackson County, 683 acres granted to said Thomas Walton in 1785, on Big Shoal Creek. Test. John H. Walton, Isham Strong and Payton Wyatt.

Nov. 24th, 1796. John Barnett to James Cooper, of Oglethorpe County, land on Oconee River. Test. Wm. M. Stokes, J.P.

Sept. 3rd, 1796. Absolom Franklin and wife, Margaret, to George Hainey, all of Franklin County, land in Jackson County. Test. Jeremiah Sparks, J.P. Urias Parks.

Dec. 1st, 1797. Zachariah Cox of Wilkes County, to Thomas Holden of Richmond Cty. land on Walnut Fork, Oconee River, Franklin County, originally granted to Cox, Sept. 20th, 1787. Test. Frederick Lipham, J. Henson. Recorded 1798.

Oct. 10, 1796. Thomas Holden of Laurens County S. C. to John Lindsey of Jackson County, land in Jackson County. Test. John Cox, John Pearson, Ezekiel Griffith.

Dec. 22nd, 1794. James Goodlet of Oglethorpe County, to John Linssey of Greene County, 143 1/4 acres, half of a bounty granted to William Quelly? Feb. 26, 1785. on Oconee River. Test. John Barnett. John Lindsey, Archibald Bryant.

July 7th, 1797. Sarah Briant, William Bond, James Bankston, to James Armstrong, Reg. of Prob. administrative bond on the estate of Benjamin Briant, late of this county, decd.

Mar. 4th, 1798. Samuel Gardner to Jos. Humphries, 30 acres on Oconee River, originally granted to Susannah Gardner and conveyed by deceased to Samuel Gardner. Test. John Espy, J.P.

Mar. 30, 1798. William Berry and Susannah, his wife, of Oglethorpe County, to Jos. Humphries of Jackson County, land on the north Oconee, surveyed for Berry. Test. Richard Hartsfield, J.P.

Dec. 5, 1797. Joseph Humphries, as adm. of the estate of Augustine Blackburn, late of this county, decd. Benjamin Vermillion, Andrew Miller, Securities. Test. James Armstrong.

June 4, 1798. William Strother and wife Elizabeth, of Oglethorpe County, to James Armstrong Sr. of Jackson County, 250 acres on Big Shoal Creek, originally granted to said Strother by Samuel Elbert, Governor. Test. Benjamin Rice, Charlton Doggett.

June 4, 1798. William Strother and wife, Jane, of Oglethorpe County, to Benjamin Rice of Jackson County, 240 acres on Big Shoal Creek, part of a 500 acre tract granted to said Strother Sept. 16th, 1785. Test. James Armstrong, Charlton Doggett. (One place shows Strother's wife as Elizabeth, another Jane)

REMNANTS OF INFERIOR COURT.

June term 1802. Joseph Hambrick applied for letters of guardianship on James Hambrick, orphan of Thomas Hambrick, Decd. Granted.

James Rogers applied for and appointed guardian to John Rogers, one of the heirs of John Rogers, Esquire, Deceased.

Petition of Frances Nail, widow of Jos. Nail, decd. to be appointed guardian of her six infant children, all under 14, viz: Ezekiel, Alexander, Kezziah, Judith, Obediah and Savoy Neal(sic), orphans of said Joseph Neal (sic). Property amounted to $4,500. Granted. Col. Roderick Easley, Jos. McCutchen, Esquire, and Thos. Kirkpatrick, Securities.

No date. Present: B. Harris, A. Rainey, M. Benge, Esquires.

The petition of Joseph Humphries for dismission as administrators of the estate of Augustine Blackburn, having advertised in the public gazette 12 months. Granted.

Aug. term 1802. Petition of Isaac Hill, Security for Swan Harden, guardian to Austine and Wm. Blackburn, heirs and representatives of Augustine Blackburn, decd., believing Swan Harden to be wasting said estate, it to be taken out of his possession. All property turned over to Isaac Hill.

John Barron praying that he may be appt. Exr. of the last will and testament of Thomas Gilleland, decd. in room(the) of Nancy Barron who was formerly the wife of said deceased.

Expenditures of Sarah Watson, a woman in the state of insanity from June 1800 to Jan. 1802. To boarding $35.00. Clothing $15.00.

Benjamin Vermillion, guardian, ditto, from Jan. 1802 to June 1802, to be paid out of money in the hands of Jos. Humphries Esq. The case settled in the August term of 1802.

On motion of John Spier and Jos. Colling Exrs. of Benjamin Cowling, decd. praying that William Loyed and Daniel Connor make title to certain lands for the benefit of the heirs. Granted.

Application of Micajah Williamson, temporary adm. of John Gorham, decd. for permanent letter. Granted. M. Nall, Clerk.

Note for $43.00 on Thomas Reynolds, in favor of Robert Campbell, decd.. ordered recorded. M. Nall, Clerk.

John A. Blackburn applies for letters of adm. on the estate of Benjamin Watson, notice having been given in one of the public gazettes. Granted.

Anderson Apperson, applied for letters of adm. on the estate of Robert Apperson, deceased. Granted.

William Satterfield of Pendleton S. C. petitions that a certain tract of land on Saluda River, Pendleton County S.C. be turned over to him, as he paid Augustine Blackburn for it in his lifetime in 1799.

WILL. Matthew Bostain. s/ Mar. 18, 1823. p/ July 1823. Wife Sarah. Son Jacob. Son Matthew. Daughters: Hannah, Elizabeth, Pwggy Bostain and Nelly J. Betts, share and Share alike. Wife Sarah and son-in-law John Betts and Richard W. Pentecost, Exrs. Test. W. Pentecost, Isaac Betts, Sr. Micajah Bennett.

WILL. Michael McDowell. / 1824? "True" last will and testament of Michael McDowell, Decd. who died Sept. 3, 1824 in Stokes County. N. C. Wife Peggy and son Allen, heirs." Test. Elizabeth Waugh, Harrison M. Waugh, Susan L. Waugh.

WILL. Zachariah Collings. p/ Mar. 1st, 1824. Wife Sarah. Sons: Abraham, John and Henry. Daughters: Eady Wallace, wife of Thompson Wallace; Rhoda Wright, wife of Elias Wright. Sarah, Elizabeth and Priscilla Collins. Mentions land expected to be drawn in present lottery. Son Abraham Exr. Test. Russell Jones, Sophia Jones and G.D. Lester.

WILL. Robert Moon. s/ Mar. 14, 1824. p/ May 3, 1824. "Some of the children under age". My three sons, William, Robert & Archibald. Exrs. Test. B. Moon, Joseph J. Scott and W.D.Martin.

WILL. Micajah Bennett. s/ Apr. 8, 1824. p/ July 5, 1824. Children: Jesse J., Jeptha, William, Peter Bennett. Sally Colton. Thomas Johnson and Richard W. Pentecost, Exrs. Test. William Pentecost. Brittain Brazeal, Josiah Bradley.

WILL. Benjamin Mayo. p/ June 7th, 1824. Wife Sally. Children to be educated. Exrs. faithful friends Joseoh Davis and Hugh Montgomery. Test. David Henderson. Elijah Oliver. Joseph Bradley.

WILL. Margaret McDowell. s/ July 1824. p/ Jan. 25, 1825. Son Allen C. McDowell. Daughters: Margaret Inelmia? McDowell, Elizabeth Caroline Boyle. James Waugh, Allen C. McDowell, David Witt. Exrs. Test H. Webb, George Shaw, J.D.Depriest.

WILL. William Heard. s/ Apr. 12, 1825. p/ Sept. 5, 1825. Wife Rachael. "Present wife's children. Daughter Sarah, only mentioned by name." 'First children' mentioned but not named. Wife Rachael and my ? Joseph Heard, Ansel Cunningham, exrs. Test. A.V.Clardy, Ansel Cunningham, James Montgomery.

WILL. Levi Wallis. s/ Dec. 17, 1824. p/ Sept. 5, 1825. Wife Jenny, life estate, to be divided between daughter Margaret and sons Josiah and Isaiah Wallis. To daughter Elizabeth Moon and son Daniel, son Thompson and the children of son, Wm. Wallis, five dollars each. Test. Henry H. Johnson, Andrew Millican, Thos. Bruce.

WILL. Samuel Langston. s/ Oct. 3, 1825. p/ Oct. 31, 1825. "Being old and infirm, my five daughters, Alcy Wright, Betsy Rhea, Rachael Williamson and Mary Blackstock. Exrs. "my friend and brethren, Edward Adams and Joseph Davis." Test. Jeremiah Reeves, John Wallis, Geo. Adams.

WILL. Michael Walling. s/ Oct. 22nd, 1825. p/ Sept. 4, 1826. Wife Lucy. Children: Priscilla, Thomas, Rachael and Hannah Walling. If they ever call for their parts, to give them one dollar. Wife Lucy and trusty friend and step-son John McNeel, Exrs. Test. Hezekiah Pruitt Arthur Mangram, Henry McNeel.

WILL. William Moore, Sr. s/ July 16th, 1827. p/ Jan. 8th, 1828. Son John Moore. Daughter Mary Borders. William Moore Borders; son of Mary Borders, son-in-law Stephen Borders and son John, Exrs. Mentions Lot No. 384, 8th, District Early

County and Lot No. 225, in the 24th, District of Lee County, "drawn by me in the last lottery." Test. M.H.Pittman, James Smith, Jos. Adair, Zachariah Lay and Thomas Johnson.

WILL. Thomas Stapler. s/ Apr. 23, 1823 p/ Mar. 6th, 1826. "Being old and crazy, but in proper mind and memory," my wife, Ruth. Daughter Sarah Owen. Daughter Mary Hutchinson. Son Amos Stapler and Joseph M. C. M. Norman, five dollars. To the children of my deceased daughter Elizabeth Norman. Daughter Frances Rogers. Daughter Rachael Strickland. Son Thomas Stapler. Son William Stapler. Daughter Nancy Rogers and her children, Elizabeth C., William S. and Sarah J. Rogers. Children of deceased daughter, Elizabeth Norman, William L., Sarah C., Polly S.,Thomas S. and Joseph G. Rogers. Granddaughter Mary Rogers. Sons Robert and Thomas Stapler, Exrs. Test. James Wilson, Thomas M. Wilson, John Sankey Riden. Zachariah Lay, Jr.

WILL. Frederick Brazeal. s/ Oct. 6th, 1821. p/ May 1, 1826. "Being old,"etc.. Wife Elizabeth Brazeal, grandsons Terrell Roberts and James Smith. Alexander Williamson. Test. Edward Adams, Martha Johnston and John Johnston.

WILL. Owen J. Bowen. s/ Aor. 7, 1825, p/Sept. 1,1828. Wife Nancy. Sons: Thos., Hiram and Perry Bowen. Daughter Thirza David.(s). Son Horatio Bowen. Freind and brother" John H. Jones, Exr. Test. John H. Jones and Absolom Spears.

WILL. James Beavers. s/ Dec. 9, 1825. p/ June 19, 1827. "Somewhat sick". Three single daughters: Martha Beavers, Jane Bishop and Mary Beavers, all my lands in Georgia and Kentucky. Test. Mary Freeman James Shields and Charity Shields.

WILL. Thomas M. Wilson. s/ Aug. 15th, 1828. p/ Nov. 3, 1828. Wife Polly, Daughter Nancy E.Wilson, child in esse, all my children. Test. Thomas Stapler, Jr, John P. Johnson, James D. Johnson, Oren Jarrett.

WILL. James Orr, Sr. s/ Apr. 15, 1828. p/ Nov. 3rd, 1828. Wife Nancy. My wife's daughter, Martha Leviston Orr, $10.00? My wife's son Thomas Orr, $10.00? To my three children: John Jr., Rebecca Wilson and Jennett Miller, all my property. Exr. John Orr, Jr. James Barr. Test. H. Webb, M. Witt, John Appleby, Edward Adams, Jr.

WILL. John Miller. s/ Nov. 20, 1828. p/ Jan. 5, 1829. Wife Mary. All property to be disposed of at her death as she pleases. Wife Mary and son William Miller Exrs. Test. Hezekiah Pruitt, Jesse Broadwell.

WILL. Josiah Henderson.s/ Oct. 7, 1828 p/ Jan. 5th, 1829. Wife Roxanna and Robt. Venable, Exrs. Property to be for the entire use of my family. Test.John Venable, Nathaniel Venable, James Green.

WILL. Thomas Millsaps. s/ Mar. 5, 1825. p/ Mar. 6, 1829. Legacies to be sons Fuller and Ezekiel Millsaps, land adjoining Jacob Millsaps on Barber's Creek, Lot No. 187 in the 13th, District of Houston Cty. The rest to be divided among all my children. Two sons named above to be Exrs. Test. Green Steed, Fanny Steed, Lewis Franklin.

WILL. Jesse Harris. s/ Mar. 22nd, 1829. p/ May 4th, 1829. Wife Viney. "My eight children", all under age. Wife Viney and friend Barnaabas Barron, Exrs. Test. Magmus A. Brooks, Walton Harris, Moses Vinson.

WILL. Samuel G. Patton. s/ Jan. 27th, 1829. p/July 6, 1829. To John and Charity Winters, slaves. All other property to sister Charity Winters and Margaret Knox heirs, when they come of age. John Winters of Jackson County and Wm. Knox of Gwinnett County, exrs. Test. James Langston, Josiah M. Kennedy, Absolom Crisler. "The note I have on Stephen Dale, I wish to be given up to him in case of my death"

WILL. Charles Damron. s/ Oct. 4, 1827. No date of probation shown. Wife Polly. Son Uriah. Daughter Polly Anglin, Daughters Nancy and Peggy Damron. Son-in-law Peter Anglin, living on certain of his lands. Son Uriah Exr. Test. Jos. J. Singleton, Asa Varnum, John Skinner.

WILL. Samuel Pool. s/ Oct. 10th, 1829. p/ Jan. 4, 1830. "Afflicted on body". All my children: John Wiley, Samuel, Drury, Seymour Spencer, Lania?, Bathena, Alice and Polly, land in Jackson, Early and Lee counties. Beloved son John Pool of Walton County, Extr. Test. Andrew J. Liddell, James Liddell, Geo. R. Grant.

WILL. Isaac Burson. s/ Sept. 28, 1829. p/ July 5, 1830. Wife Sarah. To Sylvanus Shipp and Penelope Brazeal $50.00 each. (relationship not shown) lawful heirs & wife of David Burson, decd. one dollar. My children: Joseph Burson, Hanna Thomas, Isaac Burson, Sally Hinton, Delilah Shaw [married Elijah Shaw Jackson Cty. Jan. 17, 1808], Elisha Burson and Brookfield Burson. Sons Joseph and Elisha, Exrs. Test. Wm. Shaw, John Johnson, Barnabas Johnson.

WILL. Nathaniel Legg. s/ Jan. 7, 1830. p/ Jan. 12, 1830. Wife Lucy and son Jas. M. Legg, Exrs. Property to be sold at the proper time and divided equally. Peter A. Maddux declared this to be his will. He having been present on Jan. 7, 1830. Test. Peter A. Maddux, Nathaniel Shotwell, William Legg.

EARLY COURT RECORDS

May 30th, 1797. William Tyler to David Sidwell, Sr. both of Wilkes County, 500 acres on Apalacha River. Test. John Simms and R. Worsham.

Apr. 16, 1796. Mial J. Barnett to Henry Anglin, land on Griggs Creek, originally granted to John Way Jr. 1785. s/ Mial Johnson Barnett. Polly Barnett. Test Thomas Johnson, Benjamin Parr.

May 21, 1797. John W. Zachariah Barnett Gentlemen, lands on Big Creek originally granted to John Barnett in 1797. Test. Samuel Wilkins, William Duke.

Sep. 25th, 1796. Mary Strickland and Jacob, bond as adms. on the estate of Henry Strickland, decd., late of this county. Roderick Easley, Security. James R. P. Armstrong.

Dec. 5th, 1797. Samuel Nelson to John McElhannon, both of Elbert County, land on Oconee River. Test. John Luckie, J.P.

Nov. 1, 1797. William Deakins, Jr. of Georgetown, Montgomery County Maryland, to William Lacy of Columbia County Ga. land in Franklin County, by a certain Leonard Marbury, surveyed about 1785. Test. Charles A. Beatty. Thos Corcoran.

Mar. 5, 1789. John Darden, to Phillip Guire? both of Wilkes County, land in Franklin County on Broad River. Test. Charles Finch, James Scott.

Auf. 23rd, 1797. Phillip Guire of Lincoln County, to Nathan Wright of Lincoln County, 500 acres on Broad River and Brush Creek. Test. John Gilmore, John Glaze.

June 29, 1797. John Abernathy and his H___ Clary Abernathy of Wilkes County, to William Strong of Jackson County, land on north side of Oconee River, conveyed to John Abernathy by Thomas Wooten and his wife, Tabitha June 12th, 1788. Test. John Pope, J.I.C. Gies Thomas.

Oct. 17th, 1796. John McConnell of Elbert County to James Brooks of Elbert County, land on Oconee River, part of a thousand acre grant to Thomas Barron. Test. Agnes Barr Pace. R. Pace.

Sept. 17, 1797. John Cobb of Jefferson Cty. to James Lindsey of Jackson County land in Jackson County. Test. Geo. Kenerly, Thomas Kenerly.

Feb. 10th, 1794. William McCutchen of Elbert County to Joseph McCutchen of Oglethorpe County, 300 acres on Walnut Fork, originally granted to William McCutchen in 1789. Test. J. Higganbotham.

Jan. 1, 1798. Isham Matthews to Robt. Henderson, 287 1/2 acres on Currie Creek granted Feb. 9th, 1785. Test. John King, Jos. McCutchen.

Jan. 26, 1798. James McMullen to Talbot Arthur bill of sale on household goods. Test. Wm. Nichols.

July 23, 1793. James McCamon? of Wilkes County, to Charles Dougherty of Greene County, 690 acres of Middle Fork of Oconee River, granted McCamon Dec. 31, 1787. Test. Moses Milligan, William McCree.

Dec. 1st, 1795. Charles McCartney to Charles Dougherty, both of Oglethorpe County, 358 acres, originally granted to Samuel Gardner 1785. Test. James Thomas.

Dec. 28, 1796. William M. Stokes, and his wife, Nancy, of Jackson County, to Thomas Duke Sr. of Oglethorpe County and Matthew Stone of Jackson County.

Oct. 9, 1797. Samuel Gardner to Nicholas Little, land on Sandy Creek. Test. Ezekiel Wills. James Pullman.

Feb. 7th, 1797. Archelius Jarrett & wife Martha, to James Gideon, 200 acres on Currie's Creek. Test. Thos. B. Scott, Henry West, Hezekiah Gray.

June 12, 1788. Thomas Wooten and wife Tabitha, to John Abernathy, all of Wilkes County, land on Big Shoal and Rocky Creek originally granted to said Wooten in 1786. Test. Holman Freeman, Curtis Welborn.

Oct. 24th, 1797. Charles McDonald and wife Mary, of Hancock County, to Prosser Horton of Warren County, 287 1/2 acres on Walnut Fork, Oconee River, originally granted to John Hampton and bought for taxes by McDonald.

Mar. 12, 1790. Daniel Butler of Wilkes County, to Samuel Knox of Wilkes County, land in Franklin County, originally granted to Butler Feb. 23rd, 1785. Test. J. George, Richard Woodrough.

Jan. 9, 1796. William Nichols to Saml. Knox, both of Franklin County, land on South Fork of R o c k y Creek, part of a double bounty surveyed for John Horton and adjacent lands surveyed for Knox. Test. James Barnett, J.P.

July 20, 1795. John Kinnebrew to Nicholas Long, both of Wilkes County, land in Franklin County. Test. Francis Strother. Leonard Seventyn?

Nov. 5, 1796. William Payton of Elbert County to Charles McCartney of Oglethorpe County, 250 acres on Sandy Creek. Test. J.W. Luckie, John Ponder.

Jan. 7th, 1794. James R. Whitney, T.C. of Franklin County for 1792, to John Stoddard of Abbeville, S. C. (County) the land of Barnabas Pace. Test. John Smith. Nevill Walton.

Mar. 23, 1798. Isham Williams of Jackson County, to Josiah Goolsby of Oglethorpe County, land on Oconee River. Test. James Pittman. George Taylor.

May 26th, 1797. Sydnor Cosby to David Criswell, both of Wilkes County, land on Broad River, Franklin County. Test. Daniel Price. John Symes.

REMNANTS OF INFERIOR COURT RECORDS

Probably 1798. Ambrose Cameron appt. guardian for Nancy Blackburn, minor orphan of Augustine Blackburn, Decd.

Lewis McKee bound to David Kelough.

Malachi Jones praying payment for laying out the county of Jackson, agreeable to act of assembly. Ordered he be paid $30.00. Benjamin Easley, Clerk. J. Pittman. Absolom Ramey, J.P.

Aug. 3, 1798 SESSION. Petition to lay out a road from Robert McGovern's and Daniel W. Easley's mill on north Oconee to the Middle River and across said river to Edward Williams' on Beach Crk.

A report that the road could be improved by crossing the path from Fort Madison to Vermillion, George Cowan to be overseer on the Upper District. Geo. Hampton, the middle District and Daniel W. Easley for the lower District.

A petition that a road be laid out from a road leading from Fitzpatrick's ford on the Oconee River to Harmond Reynolds, thence to Benge and Hopkins store on Barber's Creek, thence to the shoal on Beech Creek. Harmond Reynolds, Wm. Hopkins and Timothy Harris appointed Commissioners to lay it out.

Thirty dollars paid out of county fund for the support of Thomas Mackey and his wife Mary, infirm from old age. Tom Hill to receive it.

JURY DRAW FOR NEXT TERM:

Andrew Miller	Robert Williams
Lindy Harris	Daniel Allen
Simeon Lane	Thomas Webb
Joel Morton	John Smith
Asa Morgan	Theopolius Hickman
John Fielder	Sewel Holland
Robert McCord	James Knox
Allen Kelough	Wm. Tidwell Jr.
William Tidwell,Jr.	Clayborn Doss
John Ezzard	John Black
Walter Bell	David Castleberry
Joseph Lane	George Haynie
Samuel Bridgewater	John Barnett
James Nettles	William Smith
Job Tidwell	Alexa Smith
Chas. McCartney	Hugh Mairs
Jacob Pennington	James Hill
Ben Pere(Perry)	Wm. Pentecost

Agreeable to the Constitution of this State, the court proceeded to appoint a Clerk of the Court of Ordinary or Reg. of Prob. Upon counting the votes Benjamin Easley, appointed.

Inferior Court held Jan. 2, 1799. Jas. Pittman, Absolom Raimey, Buckner Harris, Esquires. Case tried, John Michael, survivor of Michael M. Simms vs. Edmond Taylor, for the plaintiff $98.12 1/2 cents.

JURY No. 1.

Asa Morgan	George Haynie
Allen Kelough	Hugh Mairs
Jacob Pennington	Walter Bell
Thomas Webb	Wm. Pentecost
Sewel Holland	Joel Morton
John Black	John Barnett

JURY No. 2

Miles Gathright	John King
Daniel Matthews	James Lindsey
Samuel Gardner	Samuel Pattern?
Joseph McCutchen	Robert Campbell
Henry Anglin	Randolph Traylor
John McCartney	Mark Nall.

COURT Jan. 3, 1799. James Pittman, Absolom Ramey, Buckner Harris, Geo. Wilson, Esq. Daniel W. Easley told the Court that five years ago, a certain heifer calf came to his house, and he called in two neighbors to value it. They did not consider it worth anything. Having raised the calf, she is now in possession of one Nathaniel Miars. The Court if of the opinion that the cow is the property of the said Daniel W. Easley.

A petition to lay out a road from the new court-house to the head branches of Black's Creek ordered done. Thomas Reynolds, John Lindsey and Geo. Wilson appt. Commissioners.

The Commissioners appointed to lay out the road from Candler's Creek to the Sulphur Spring, reported they have done so. The Court ordered it cleared and Robert Williams, William Deal and Wm. Moore appointed Commissioners. [Road builders of ye olden times]

The Commissioners appointed to lay out the road from Sexton ford on the Oconee River, to the Cherokee Corner, reported they have laid out said road. Isaac Middlebrooks & John Malone appointed overseers.

Commissioners appointed to lay out a road from the Furnace to the new courthouse, report they have marked out the same. Bryant Mooney, Henry Cook and Park Chandler appointed Commissioners.

Clerk of Superior Court made his returns. Estrays sold 1798. $6.00.

Charlton B. Scroggins allowed license to sell spiritous liquors.

Paid Ben Easley for services as Clerk of Inferior Court, $51.75.

Thomas Hutson appointed Costable in Capt. Cunningham's District. Ben Parr in Capt. Traylor's District. William Moore, Jr. and Bryant Mooney in Capt. Reynold's District. Andrew Miller in Capt. Keloughs District. The old Constables in the other Districts.

The Clerk ordered to call upon the T.C. for the taxes of 1797 and 1798. If not paid, issue an execution. Ordered that James Harper, Esquire, surveyor for the county, be paid $40.00 for the purpose of fixing the p u b l i c buildings; and his chain bearers $19.00, to-wit: Robert McGowan, Jacob Lindsey and Jacob Summerlin.

Feb. 4, 1799. James M. Pittman, Absollom Ramey, Buckner Harris, Esquires. Robt McAlpin asks t h a t a road be continued from a road leading to Greensborough to the long shoal on the Apalacha where the said road strikes the county line, to the long s h o a l and to be continued to the courthouse. Ratford Ellis, Stephen Nobles Micajah Benge and Joseph Clarkston appt. Commissioners. Ordered a road layed out from Dooley Shoal on the Big Pond fork to the new courthouse. John Hill, William Humphries and John Shields, Commrs.

JURORS FOR THE NEXT COURT:

James Henderson
William Parsons
John Brown
George Humphries
David Kelough
Peter Tidwell
John Shields
Isaac Tidwell
Littleberry Epperson
Jas. Kirkpatrick
James Miller
John Kinderly
Edward Phillips
Isaac Middlebrooks
John Nall
Absolom Tidwell
John Reynolds
Buck Ledbetter
John Moss
Thomas Nichols
Richard Wyatt
John Wood
Thomas Brown
Samuel Knox
Daniel Kelough
James Tuttle, Jr.
James Kelough
Jacob Lindsey
Geo. Wilson Jr.
Wm. Stinson
Samuel Parks
Thos. Hightower
Derby Handley
James Scott
Samuel Pattern
Charles Smith

Mar. 5th, 1799. William Pace and James Stewart allowed license to retail liquors B. Easley, Clerk.

Mar 9th, 1799. The Clerk of this Court ordered to call on James Armstrong, Reg. of Prob. for all books and documents relative to Court of Ordinary, to have them present before the first Monday in April.

Apr. 1st, 1799. This Court for the purpose of nominating Justices in several Districts of the county, to-wit: William Strong, John Cunningham, District No. 1. Paul Patrick, Randolph Traylor, District No. 2. Joseph East, Samuel Gardner, District No. 3. John McFalls, Martin Nall, Districy No. 4. John Espy, Miles Gathright, District No. 5. Robert McAlpin, Henry Trent, District No. 6. Thomas Rogers & William Carter, District No. 7. Thomas Joseph McCutchen, District No. 8. Abner Bankston, Gabriel Hubbard, District No. 9. Robert Easley, Peter Kolb, District No. 10. H u g h Montgomery, James Porter, District No. 11. John McConnell, John Diamond, District No. 12. Thomas Brown, John Smith, District No. 13. William Pentecost, Ethelred Wood, District No. 14. SIGNED George Wilson, Absolom Ramey. B. Harris, John Hampton, James Pittman.

Issued license for retailing spiritous liquors to John Malone a n d Robert Campbell, and Witt and Billups.

Apr. 4th, 1799. The Inferior Court made the following appointments: Ordered that the C l e r k advertise the building of a jail, to be let to the lowest bidder on the first Saturday in May next at Clarksboro. The plan of said house is as follows. Twenty-two feet square on the outside, two-story high, a single roof. The f i r s t story to begin two feet in the ground, built with a double wall of hewn timbers, at least 10 inches square, and filled with small round poles end-ways so as to make the two walls three feet thick to be eight feet clear in the pitch. The floor to begin even with the surface of the earth, layed with hewn timbers a foot thick close together, then with two-inch oak planks nailed down with spikes within six inches of each other. The second floor in the same manner and a trap door in the middle, three feet square well ironed. The second stpry to be a 10 foot pitch in the clear and only the out-wall carried up The upper floor of squared timbers six in. thick. A door to the upper story well ironed and the eight tight glass windows well grated; the lower floor to have two windows eight inches square grated in and out Ordered that Thomas Hill, Edmund Edwards and William Robertson be Commissioners to keep the Oconee River clear in this county.

July 6th, 1799. Payments on the jail to be made, draft on Tax Coll. of Taxes, for 100 dollars this year;$40.00 to be paid the 25th, day of December due from the sale of Public l o t s. The rest out of the first funds raised in the county and the jail to be completed by April 1st, next.

Knocked off to Jett Thomas $797.00 beginning bond and security for completion.

Justices of the county also qualified on this day: William Daniel qualified as Tax Collector and Jacob Lindsey as Receiver of Taxes.

Aug. 1st, 1799. Court opened in due form a n d adjourned to the new courthouse at Clarksboro ten o'clock tomorrow.

Clarksboro Aug. 2, 1799. Jury No. 1.
James Kirkpatrick   John Lindsey
James Miller   David Kelough
John Nall   John Kenerly
John Reynolds   Samuel Parks
Wm. Stinson   James Kelough
Samuel Pattern   Jacob Lindsey

Daniel W. Easley vs. George a n d John McFalls, judgement for $68.66 1/4 cents. Francis Goodon and company vs. Jacob Carter, judgement for. plaintiff $17.79 and cost.

Talbot Arthur vs. William Hutchinson, judgement for t h e plaintiff $60.00 with cost.

The Executors of Anthony Ollive vs. Robt Campbell. Parties mutually agree to submit all matters to James Pittman, Isaac Hill, John Hampton, Thomas Johnson a n d Samuel Gardner.

Saturday Aug. 3, 1799. A road to be laid out from Joseph Clarkson's? to the Skull Shoals. George Harper, Timothy Harris and William Watkins, Commissioners appointed to lay out a road from Beech Creek to the c o u n t y line joining a road leading to Fitzpatrick's Ferry report their work done The same to be cleared a n d Luke Durbin, overseer, to clear f r o m Beech Creek to Gabriel Hubbard, James Stringer to Benges store, and Jesse Jenkins to Col. Runnells and William Bankston to the county line

Tax Collector ordered to pay Jett Thomas o n e hundred dollars towards building the. jail.

Micajah Williamson appointed overseer of the poor.

Ordered that J o h n Freeman, jailer at Hancock C o u n t y be allowed $72,77 for keeping William H o d g e, a prisoner and citizen of Jackson County.

Samuel Bridgewater paid $19.53 as per account rendered for services for executing two Negroes, and board.

Robert Bailey, James Glenn a n d John King, surveyors for road from courthouse to head of Black= Creek.

Charles Dougherty, Esquire, Sheriff, allowed $72.30 for sundry expenses of Wm. Hodge, a prisoner who was executed. The guards to be allowed the sums annexed to their names as follows: Robert Tucker $3.75. James McMillen $4.50. Anderson Foster $14.25. Rice Simpson $14.25. Thos. Kelough $14.25. James Stewart allowed $10.35 for boarding the guards over Wm. Hodge, a prisoner. David Ray, a witness against William Hodge, allowed $4.50.

Relief granted Moses Sandreth, an infirm man.

Thomas Kirkpatrick, John Diamond and John Hill, appointed Commissioners to lay out a road from the courthouse to where the Stone road crosses Middle River.

John Nall, David Robertson and Edward Williams, appointed surveyors for the road leading from Cedar Shoal to Beech Creek.

Road from Easley's mill on Cedar Shoal to Cherokee corner, to be layed out. Charles Dougherty, Talbot Arthur & Catt. D. Scroggins appointed Commissioners.

Road laid out from Pope's ford on the north Oconee by Espy's Mill and to the road from Chandlers to Sulphur Springs. Samuel Gardner, James Glenn and John Parks appointed Commissioners.

William Melton allowed $9.32 for moving William Hodge, a prisoner, to this cty.

Following persons appointed overseers of the road: Richard Hopkins, from the county line to Squire McAlpin's; Thomas Shannon, from thence to Call's Creek. Thomas Currie, from thence to his house, Currie and Robert McGowan, from thence to town.

Clerk to make out and direct to James Armstrong, to being all books, etc. connected with his office of Reg. Prob.b6f before the Court of Ordinary, to be held the first Tuesday in September. Tax levied equal to one-fourteenth of the general tax for the benefit of the poor. The overseer not to give anyone applicant over ten dollars at a time.

The following men drawn as jurors failed to appear and answer to their names, fined five dollars each: Isaac Middlebrooks, John Wood, Samuel Knox, Isaac Treadwell, S. David Kelough, John Moss and Thos. Hightower.

Moses Shears, Esquire, paid twenty dollars, twelve and one half cents, for bringing William Hodge, a criminal, to this place.

NO DATE. Ephriam Lindsey, guardian of John McElroy, returns.

Thomas McCain of Wilkes County, in his lifetime, under date of 1785, gave bond for title to 287 1/2 acres to Holman Freeman. Samuel Henderson, the assignee of Freeman, prays that Abraham Warren, adm. of Thomas McCain, give good titles. Test. Francis Woodward.

FROM DEED BOOK A - B

June 20, 1794. Henry Carlton, of Wilkes County, to William Puryear and Susannah Cox of ? "Dogwood Grove tract" on Cedar Creek surveyed by John Gorman in 1785 for Walker Richards, the tract to be equally divided between Wm. Puryear and Susannah Cox. Five hundred pounds paid them. Test. Gabriel Carlton and B. Christmas.

Dec. 2, 1794. Nicholas Hawkins of Oglethorpe County, to James Freeman of Greene County, 525 acres on Shoal Creek. Test J. Humphries. Surveyed as bounty grant for heirs of James Hawkins Apr. 7, 1789.

June 10th, 1794.. Charles Dougherty to Jeremiah Matthews, both of Oglethorpe cty, land in Franklin County on Middle Fork of Oconee River, originally granted to said Dougherty Dec. 1, 1787. Test. Jas. Thomas.

[Several Earmarks recorded in same deed book, as follows]

July 6th, 1796. Mary Kelough. David Kelough, Sr., David Kelough, Jr. George Taylor. William Deal. Sept. 12, 1796. Receipt of Philemon Martin, Tax Collector for Henry Potts' Tax. Earmarks, Johnson Clark and Joseph East. Jan. 5, 1797. John Black and John Seals, James Armstrong, Martha Patton

MISCELLANEOUS RECORDS JACKSON COUNTY GEORGIA

Jan. 6, 1797. William Duke, Josiah Morton. John Jones. Apr. 8, 1797. Jonothan Jones. Robert Barker, Joseph Clarkston. May 1st, 1797, Alexander Morrison, Henry Ledbetter. Aug. 4, 1797. John Barron. Sept. 14, 1797. Joseph Humphries. Dec. 17, 1797. Roderick Easley.

Dec. 16, 1793. William Owens to Lawrence Biers? both of Wilkes County, 230 acres in Franklin County, originally granted to John Lynch in 1784.

Mar. 25, 1794. John Depriest and wife, Jane, to Elisha Johnstand, all of Elbert County, land in Franklin County, originally granted to Peter Oliver. Test. John Rogers, J.P.

Jan. 22, 1795. John Wyatt and wife Mary, to Jonas Short, all of Oglethorpe County, 150 acres on Shoal Creek. Test. Thomas Price and John Griffin.

Nov. 15, 1796. David McCleskey and Thos. Rogers of Elbert County, to Thomas Hemphill of Burke County N. C., 200 acres on Currie's Creek, part of a tract originally granted to William Longstreet in 1786. Sold to John Boston, to John H. Johnson, to said David McCleskey. Test. John Luckie of Oglethorpe County. Mary McCleskey and Martha Rogers renounce their dower Nov. 6, 1796.

Oct. 29, 1796. John H. Johnson, to David McCleskey and Thomas Rogers, 200 acres on Currie's Creek. Test. John Connell, Samuel Nelson.

Oct. 3, 1796. Hugh Mains and wife, Jane, to George Smith, 40 acres on Briggs Creek, adjacent to land of Smith. Test. George Taylor, J.P.

Oct. 3, 1796. William Deal and wife, Jemima to George Smith, land on Trail Creek. Test. George Taylor.

Nov. 21, 1796. Daniel W. Easley to Rodericy Easley, sale of slaves, cattle, etc. Test. George Taylor, William Streetman.

Oct. 7, 1794. James McCommon and William McCree to Geo. Calhoun, all of Oglethorpe County, 225 acres on north fork of Oconee River, granted to Zachariah Cox Nov. 1788, conveyed to Cox to McCommon and McCree September 1790. Test. John Humphries, J.P.

Apr. 7th, 1796. James McCommon, heirs of estate of late McCommon of Oglethorpe Cty. to George Cohoon of Greene County, land on south fork of Broad River, granted 1790 to said James McCommon. Signed Susannah McCommon, John McCommon, Margt. McCommon. Test. James Thomas.

Sept. 13, 1794. Isaac Milligan of Wilkes County to George Cohoon of Oglethorpe Cty. 200 acres on Barber's Creek, part of a survey of 287 acres to Richard Levins, granted Dec. 1788, conveyed by James Levin the lawful heir of said Levin, to Isaac Milligan, July 5, 1791. Test. William McCree, William Milligan.

July 28, 1798. Jeremiah Matthews and wife Sarah, to Elijah Hendon, all of Oglethorpe County, 300 acres, originally granted to Charles Dougherty in 1787. Test. A. Bell.

Aug. 7, 1796. Andrew Bell of Oglethorpe County, to Isham Hendon, ditto, lands on Oconee River, Jackson County, originally granted to John Rosson in 1787. Test. John Holmes, Elijah Hendon.

July 6th, 1796. Samuel Gardner, to John Cunningham, land on Cedar Creek, both sides, north fork of Oconee River. Test. William M. Stokes.

Sept. 18, 1793. Samuel Gardner of S.C. to John McCartney, May 5, 1786. Test. Wm. Hitchcock, Jesse Hitchcock, Proved in Oglethorpe County June 28, 1794.

June 7th, 1793. James McCommon and Wm. McCree and Thomas Good of Wilkes County, part of a grant to Zachariah Cox in 1788. Test. John McCutchen. Wm. Robbentsonn.

May 4, 1796. Joseph Morton of Oglethorpe County to Arthur Patton of Jackson County land on Big Shoal Creek, part of a grant to Thomas Wooten in 1786, conveyed by him to Joseph Morton in 1791. Test. John Barnett.

Agreement. John Towns and John Depriest that Towns relinquish all claims to 287 1/2 acres which the grant of Joseph Gunnells covers. "If my grant should hold the lands of mine". Test. Andrew Cunningham.

Oct. 10th, 1796. Josiah Woods and wife Sally of Franklin County, to Isaac Hill of Wilkes County Ga., 460 acres, part of a tract of 690 acres granted said Woods in 1791. William Johnson.

Jan. 29th, 1797. Robert Campbell to Wm. Park, land on Crooked Creek.

Feb. 6, 1797. Robert Campbell, to Jeremiah McCarter, land on Crooked Creek, all land originally granted to Daniel Gardner and conveyed by him to Robert Campbell.

May 7, 1796. John Garnett, of Richmond County, to Jacob Hoover of Jackson County land on Sandy Creek. Test. Wm. Daniel and Daniel Taylor.

Feb. 14, 1797. John Towns of Wilkes Cty. to James Parks of Jackson County, 250 acres on Cabin Creek. Test. Claborn Crawford.

June 9th, 1795. Russell Jones and wife, Sarah, to Robert Parks, all of Oglethorpe County, 287 1/2 acres in Franklin County, known as the Indian Cabins, originally granted to John Rench 1785. Test. James Parks and Isham Davis.

Oct. 30, 1791. John Hinson of Greenville County S. C., to Dennis McFall of Wilkes County, granted to Hinson July 31, 1788 on the waters of Oconee River, Franklin Cty. Test. Edmond Taylor. John Allison.

Feb. 11th, 1797. Thomas Scott of Elbert County, to Mordecai Benton, 1,150 acres on Turkey Creek. Test. B. Smith. Jas. Simms.

May 13th, 1794. Dennis McFall to George McFall, both of Oglethorpe County, land on Oconee River, part of Henson tract. Test. Byers, Sr. William Byers Jr.

May 6th, 1796. Garnett[Garrett?] John of Richmond County, to Isham Matthews of Jackson County. Test. Daniel Matthews and William Daniel.

Jan. 9, 1797. Robert Campbell to Samuel Park, land on north fork, Oconee River, originally granted to Samuel Gardner. Test Samuel Gardner, William Park, Geo. Taylor.

William Barnett, adm. of William Barnett decd. applied Aug. 30th, 1796 in Columbia County to sell 287 1/2 acres in Franklin County on Indian Creek, sells it to John Maddux. Test. J. Smith. Peter Crawford.

John Henson to Josiah N. Kennedy, all of Greenville County, S. C., land in Franklin County. Test. J. McGehee, Joshua Kennedy.

Mar. 5, 1789. Mordecai Benton to William George, land on Turkey Creek, Franklin County, part of original grant to Robert Middleton. Test. John Depriest, James Depriest. Proved by the oath of John Depriest in Jackson County in 1798.

Aug. 31, 1798. William Hopkins and Micajah Benge to William Watkins, land on Barber's Creek. Test. Josiah McDonald and John Hopkins.

Aug. 9, 1798. William Daniel of Elbert County, attorney for John Garnett, of Augusta, Richmond County, to William Carter, Esquire, of Jackson County, land on Sandy Creek. Test. Alexander Morrison and Allen Daniel.

Jan. 10, 1794. James Whitney, Tax Collector of Franklin County, to Russell Goodrich of Cahrleston S.C., 1,150 acres Test. Wm. J. Hobby. George Henning.

Oct. 28th, 1796. Isaac Perry of Burke County, to John Barnett of Jackson Cty. 345 acres on Currie Creek granted to Jeremiah Bentley Sept. 16, 1785, then in Franklin County, now in Jackson County. Test. James Brown. Timothy Harris.

Nov. 6, 1798. Abednego Moore and John Webb of Jackson County, to Richard Sappington of Wilkes County, 200 acres in Montgomery County, N.C. on Glady fork of Beaver Dam Creek. Signed Abednego Moore.

A n n Moore, John Webb, Elizabeth Webb. Test. Randolph Traylor, Archelius Braynt.

July 19th, 1791. William Hunt, Jr. of Richmond County Ga. to John Jack, blacksmith, of Greene County, 287 1/2 acres in Franklin County, granted to said Hunt in 1788. Test. Thomas Hunt. Thomas White

Nov. 9, 1798. John Jack and wife, Mary to Owen J. Bowen, 287 1/2 acres bounded southeast by Hawkins. All other sides vacant at time of survey. Test. Martha McGehee, Andrew Baxter.

Nov. 20, 1798. James Freeman, to Owen J. Bowen, both of Oglethorpe County, land in Jackson County on Oconee River. Said land in the grant to be on Shoal Creek, 575 acres surveyed for Nicholas Hawkins by Joseph McCutchens and granted in a bounty to the heirs of Jas. Hawkins Apr. 7, 1798. Test. Burwell Pope.

Oct. 3rd, 1791. John Wood, of Chatham County, to John McGraw of Maryland, 344 acres on Beech Creek, Franklin County, part of a tract of 600 acres originally granted to said Wood March 3rd, 1786. s/ William Moore and I. Few.

Jan. 12, 1798. Henry Chandler of Warren County to David Castleberry of Jackson County, land in Franklin, now Jackson County. Test. Test. Richard Castleberry. Thomas Castleberry.

Oct. 7th, 1797. James R. Whitney, Tax Collector, Jackson County, to Daniel W. Easley of Jackson County. Test. John Bostick and Moses Payne.

Dec. 1, 1798. Eleazar Mobley, deed of gift to friend, Ruth Glover, slaves, at his death or upon their separation. Upon her death to descend to Jethro Mobley's children. Test. E. Hargrove, Howell Runnolds.

July 22, 1791. Payton Wyatt and wife, Hannah Clark Wyatt, to Bedford Brown, originally granted to said Wyatt 1790. (no counties listed). Test. Wm. Bibb.

Dec. 24, 1798. Bedford Brown to Valentine Guiger, land in Franklin County, originally granted to Payton Wyatt 1790. Test. Oliver Prince, D. Hillhouse.

Dec. 4, 1798. George Weatherby of Jefferson County, to Harmond Reynolds of Jackson County, land on Big Pond fork of Oconee River. Test. E. Hargrove. E.C. Mobley.

Oct. 15th, 1798. William Head, to Wm. Robison, of Oglethorpe County, land in Jackson County. Test. Elijah Hendon and George Wray.

Dec. 28th, 1798. Arthur Crawford of Oglethorpe County, to William Robertson of Jackson County. Test. Wm. Campbell, John Robison.

Mar. 21, 1797. John Garrett of Augusta Richmond County, to Matthew Knight of the same place, but late of London. Test. John McGowan, John Galloway. Catherine, wife of John Garrett, releases her right of dower.

Dec. 28th, 1798. Philemon Martin, Tax Collector of Franklin County, to Eldridge Hargrove, land in Franklin County, originally granted to John Turner and sold as property of Abner Jones. Test. John Martin. Drury Harrington.

Oct. 21, 1793. Micajah Williamson, Jr. of Wilkes County, to Lamech Hudson of Wilkes County. Test. A. Lipman. R. Christmas.

WILL. John Martin Carter. s/ Jan. 6, 1802. p/ Feb. 3rd, 1803. Wife Elizabeth, sole heir and Exr. Wit. B. Harris, M. Williamson, Richard Easley.

WILL. Nathan McGehee. s/ Aug. 15, 1802 p/ Feb. 3, 1803. Son Nathan, five shillings. My four sons: Jesse, Robert, Osborn and Solomon McGehee, and son Mial McGehee. Daughter Patsy McGehee. (wife not mentioned). Test. J o h n Shepherd, John Chapman, Abraham Chandler, Gabriel Anderson.

WILL. William Deal. s/ July 23, 1802. p/ Apr. 24, 1804. Wife Jemima. "My children". Wife Jemima, Ephriam a n d Jarvis Deal, Exrs. Test. James Goodlet, Richard Gardner.

WILL. William Newton. s/ Oct. 15, 1802. p/ Apr. 23, 1804. To my mother Mary Newtom all property and part of my father's estate that was coming to me in Orange County, N. C. All my accounts, etc., to mu aunt Jane Eakin. Uncle Samuel Eakin and mother Mary Newton, Exrs. Test. Adly Alexander and George Eakin.

WILL. Robert Beavers. s/ Jan. 12, 1805. p/ Jan. 28th, 1805. Wife Jane, home on Buffalo Creek, etc. Oldest daughter Esther Hunt. Daughter Rachael Brooks, daughter Polly Freeman. Daughters: Patsy, Elizabeth, Sally a n d Charity Beavers. Sons: Joseph, Reuben, John and Silas Beavers. Two daughters Betsy and Charity $15.00. I am to receive for helping Sarah Watson for the trouble they have had with her. Exrs. Son Reuben Beavers. Test Ezekiel Strickland, Solomon Strickland, William Headen.

WILL. John Berry. s/ Oct. 8, 1803. p/ Jan. 28th, 1805. Wife Martha. "My five children: Joshua, Robert, William, Mary, and Elizabeth Berry. Test. Thos. Camp, Thomas Willingham, Gideon Thomason.

WILL. Johnston Clark. s/ Sept. 3, 1805. p/ Mar. 3, 1806. Wife Sarah, son James, home plantation equally divided between them. Daughters: Hannah Henderson a n d Patsy Clark. Sister Ann Freeman, $10.00, if she is alive. (Patsy still in school) Exrs. Thomas Ewing, David McCurdy. Test. Richard Gideon, Alexa McNaughton, Jonothan Pharr.

WILL. John Wright. s/ June 3, 1803. p/ May 5th, 1806. Wife Ayle. "Beloved dtr. Aletha York?" "My beloved children" Sally, Hannah, Reek, Cornelius, Patsy and Cassey. To Jonothan Dreadon, $100.00 in case of his fulfilling servitude. Exrs. Gen. David Dickson. James Pittman a n d Jos. Davie. Test Jos. Reed, Cornelius and Mary McCarty.

CODICIL: Having a son born since the making of this will, want him to have a share with the other children. (Called wife Elsy. Mary 29, 1806). Test. Cornelius McCarty. Benjamin Whorton, James Rogers.

WILL. William Allen. s/ Aug. 25, 1806. p/ Oct. 26, 1806. "Mow and weak in body" Wife Elizabeth. My four sons: William, (only one mentioned). Test. Edward Adams and Reuben Beavers.

WILL. Henry Walker. s/ Aug. 2nd, 1806. p/ Jan. 6, 1807. Wife Christian. Daughters: J a n e Paulson, Elizabeth Hewett, Martha Shipp. Eldest son Jonothan Walker Sons: John, William and Elethen Walker, Lot No. 125, 3rd, District Baldwin Cty. drawn by me, Wife Christian, son Elethen Son-in-law Wm. Shipp, Exrs. Test. James McDonald, Ethelred Wood, Wm. Miller.

WILL. Michael Borders. s/ Sept. 7th, 1804. p/ Jan. 6, 1807. "Very sick" Wife Mary. Daughters: Esther Graham, Rachael Hixon, Mary Ann Click. Phoebe and Ruth Borders. Sons: Isaac, John and Stephen Borders. Exrs. Wife Mary and John Borders. Test. James Rogers, Thomas Johnson.

WILL. George Bagby. s/ Feb. 21, 1806. p/ July 7, 1807. Wife Miriam. Sons: Jos., Thomas a n d Abner, Henry, William and George Washington Bagby. Three youngest sons under age, Henry, Wm. and Washington. Daughters: Sally Wood, Rachael Shears and youngest daughter Betsy Jeffries Bagby. Exrs. Wife Miriam; sons John and Joseph. Test. William and Delilah Pentecost.

WILL. John Green. s/ Apr. 22, 1807. p/ Nov. 2, 1807. "Sick"-Wife Jane. Sons Wm. and John Green, under age. Daughters: Margaret, Matilda and Sarah Green, lot No. 383, First District of Wayne County, Test. John J. Mobley, James and John Wilson.

WILL. William Headen, Sr. s/ Nov. 24, 1807. p/ Jan. 4, 1808. Wife Jane. Sons: Robert, William, George, Eli and Jesse Headen. Son-in-law William Shed. James

Robertson, David Robertson, William L. Brazeal and Allen Headen. To Elizabeth, wife of John Headen and to Sally Terrell my granddaughter, five cents each.

Daughter Prissy Headen. Exrs. Son Wm. and George Headen. Test. Edward Adams, John Beavers and Reuben Beavers.

WILL. George Headen. s/ 1819. p/ Jan. 24th, 1829. "My four nephews: John M., George R. and William C. C. and Headen Brazeal." Brother William Headen, brother-in-law David Robertson, brother-in-law Wm. Shed. Brothers-in-law James Turner, Henry Turner, one part to be in the hands of John M. Brazeal for the use of Jesse Headen, James Robertson, Eli Headen, equal parts. Six heirs of Wm. L. Brazeal, viz: Sally and Polly Brazeal, and four boys. Exrs. Friend Edward Adams Nephew, John M. Brazeal. Test. Ezekiel Green, James Boring and John Boring.

WILL. Janett Beard. s/ Jan. 23, 1806. p/ Sept. 5, 1808. "Low state of health", Daughters: Elizabeth and Jean. Younger sons George and Thomas. Eldest sons, Wm. and Alexander Beard. George and Thomas, under age. Exrs. Wm. and Alexander Beard Test. Mary Beard, James Barr, Claborn Castleberry.

WILL. Jacob Whitworth. s/Oct. 12,1811. p/ Feb. 12, 1812. (a planter from S.C.). " Having acquired by purchase and otherwise,property,real and personal, in S.C. Ga. and elsewhere, to my be,oved wife, for her own, and my childrens' support, to be equally divided among them as they come of age. Son Samuel W. Whitworth and Richard Watts, Exrs. Test. Owen J. Bowen Isaac Linch and Michael Dickson.

WILL. Thomas Hanson, Jr. Nun-cupative. p/ March 2nd, 1812. "After a settlement with my brother, John Hanson, my father, Thomas Hanson, sole heir". Affidavit by David Rogers that he was with Thomas Hanson in his last sickness - Nov. 13th, 1811 - and at his death, and the above will was what he wished done.

WILL. Ann Angel. s/ Mar. 18th, 1812. p/ May 4, 1812. All estate to her five grand daughters: Cynthia Lee, Tabitha Pierce, Harriett Christian, Louisiana and Martha Gibson Johns, daughters of Bartlett Johns Mentions tract of 132 acres in Jackson County, bought of Sarah Cowan. All to be divided when the youngest comes of age. Son-in-law Bartlett Johns, sole exr. Test Horation W e b b. Bartlett C. and Phebe Johns.

WILL. George Bradford. [Yeoman]. May(s), 17th, 1812. p/ July 6, 1812. "Very sick". Wife Mary. Daughter Nancy Bradford, unmarried. Sons: William, David, George and James. Exrs. Sons William and David. Test Early Harris, Jesse Thompson, D.H.McCleskey.

WILL. Elijah Cowan. s/ Feb. 8, 1810. p/ July 6th, 1812. Wife Prudence. Sons: Wm. Edward and Stephen Cowan, as they come of age. [Wife Prudence Stovall]/ Test. Ambrose Blackwell, Agnes Blackwell, David Dickson.

WILL. James Smith, Sr. p/ Mar. 1, 1812. Daughters: Polly, Nancy and Anna. Sons: William and Samuel, a horse in possession of Nicholas Jarrett, to be given to his son, James Jarrett, which is to be deducted out of Nicholas Jarret's legacy at my wife, Ann's, death. John, James and Silas Smith, exrs. Test. Wm. Ellington, Wm. Hancock and James Glenn.

WILL. Mrs. Martha Cureton. Nun-cupative p/ Apr. 13, 1813. Has died today and left no will. That she be buried by her husband at Mrs. Chandler's. Mr. James Rogers ro preach her funeral. Her bed to Polly, Wood, daughter of James Wood, decd. Some clothes to Patsy Anderson and her little sisters. Feather bed to Taylor Whatley. That H u g h Montgomery to attend to all and get Mingo and keep him and Lett together as long as they live, if in his power. That her husband's grave be paled in with $2.00. Mr. McNess owes her. Signned Tabitha Chandler. Test.Thos.Niblack.

WILL. James Carrel. s/ Mar. 9, 1813. p/ July 6, 1813. Wife Sarah, my five children. Land granted to John Tidwell in the 12th, District of Wilkinson County, Ga. ditto to Nan? Loftin, 20th, District Wilkinson County, part of several tracts in York County, S.C. granted to John Carrel, John Humphries and James Keytendale. Test John Miller, Wm. Fowler, Elijah Robey.

WILL. William Castleberry. s/ Nov. 15, 1812. p/ ,ay 12th, 1813. Wife Lucretia, property to her during her widowhood. If she marries, to be divided among the five youngest children. Test. Elijah Robey. Mark Castleberry. Odiam? Castleberry.

WILL. Charles Waetherford. s/ Mar. 18, 1814, p/ Nov. 7, 1814. "Feeble in body". Wife Charity. Children: Archibald Weatherford, Rhoda Armstrong, Patsy Carr, Betsy Hooks and Susey Hare. Exr. Solomon Townsend. Test. James H. McEwen, Martha McEwen and Bartlett Walker.

WILL. Peter Boyle. p/ Feb. 21st, 1814. Wife Hannah to live on the farm, formerly occupied by Thomas Townsend. Sons: Robert, John, Peter, all lands originally owned by Henry Townsend and Wm. Malone. Daughter Rebecca, land in Hancock County, on Shoulder Bone Creek. Daughter Catherine, youngest daughter & grandson Bishop Clements. Hugh Montgomery, Edward Adams and son, John, Exrs. Test. Joseph David, James Armour, William Armour.

WILL. Alexander Harper. s/ Oct. 15th, 1813. p/ March 6th, 1815. Wife Tabitha. Daughters Martha a n d Elizabeth Harper. Son Alexander F. Harper, not of age. Wife Tabitha a n d Joseph Davis, exrs. Test. Joseph McCutchen, Elizabeth Echols and Martha Harper.

WILL. James Elmore. Nun-cupative. Dec. 1st, 1814, who died yesterday (Oct. 28, 1814), said to Benjamin and Wm. Whorton? that William Pinson was to have a slave. To James M. Swain, an orphan boy in N.C. a slave. All other property to Simeon White, provided said Elmore did not marry before his death and continue to live with said White.

WILL. Henry Stoneham. s/ Sept. 9, 1814 p/ July 3rd, 1815. Wife Jane. Children: Mary, Susannah, Henry, Jane, John, Wm., Elizabeth, Martha, James a n d Sophia, Esther Bryant a n d Erastus Stoneham, a feather bed each. Sons George and Joseph the children under age. John Espy, Thos. Hughes, George and Joseph Stoneham, Exrs. Test. John Cash, Edmond Roberts, Joseph Maddox.

WILL. Joseph Culpepper. s/ Jan. 15th, 1816. p/ May 6,1816. Wife Nancy. Children Simeon, Henry and Sally Culpepper. Wife a n d son Simeon and Ambrose Yarborough, Exrs. Test. Thomas J. Bowen, John Hogan, Ambrose Yarborough.

WILL. James Orr. s/ Aug. 20th, 1810, p/ May 6th, 1816. Wife Ealse. To the five children of my niece Sarah Love, twenty five cents each. Wife Ealse and David Dickson, Sr. Exrs. Test Michael Dickson, Benjamin Echols and Isaac R. Dyke.

WILL. John Adams. s/ July 1st, 1816. p/ July 30th, 1816. "To friend James Cowan, all my slaves, at whose death they are to be carried to come part of the U.S, or alesewhere where they may be free", James and Isaac Cowan, Exrs. Test. Hosea Camp, David S. McCrary and Geo. Headen.

WILL. William Hickman. s/ May 15, 1816. p/ Sept. 2nd, 1816. Wife Lucretia. Sons: Josiah, William, Theopolius, Nathaniel a n d Jacob Hickman. Daughters Lucretia Holland, Sarah Castleberry, Tamar Whitmore, Jenny Dunn, Usby? Grantham, Uphe? Mooney. Mourning Heath a n d Christianna Thomas. Son Josiah and son-in-law Richard H e a t h, Exrs. Test. Frederick Brazeal, Joseph Davis and Josiah Hickman.

WILL. James Gideon Jr. s/ June 6, 1803. p/ Aug. 4, 1817. Wife Elizabeth, the home farm to be rented till sons Hosea and Berry come of age. Other children [names not given] Prosser Horton and William McCutchen, Exrs. Test. Robert Martin, Saml, Henderson and Ben McCleskey.

WILL. Nathan Fowler. Sept. 14, 1815. p/ July 7, 1817. "Old and infirm" Two oldest children, Tabitha and Zepheniah. Son Hillory, daughter Eleshba Rowland. Daughter Eliphalet Jones' children. Daughter Abisha Beauchamp. Isaac Cowan, Exr. Test. Wiley Pierce, Medley White, William Green and Isaac Cowan.

WILL. John Coleman. s/ Apr. 3, 1816. p/ Jan. 5, 1818. Everything to wife, Elizabeth Coleman. Test. Nancy Combs, Mary Combs, George Shaw.

WILL. Shadrack Deen. s/ May 11, 1811. p/ Mar. 1, 1813. Wife Mourning. Children under age. Sons: Arche, Thomas, Jacob, Shadrack, John and Frederick. Daughter Eupharance. Son, Shadrack, Exrs. Test. Owen J Bowen, William Mackie, Jonothan Martin and Sion Pritchett.

WILL. Joseph Scott, Sr. s/ Nov. 15th, 1817. p/ Jan. 6, 1818. Wife Susannah. Son Joseph. Daughter Catey Shields. Daughter Esther Easley. Children of my daughter, Margorie Cowan. Son-in-law Isaac Cowan. Son Joseph J. a n d William Potts, Exrs. Test. Edward Adams, Claborn Harris, Wm. Combs.

WILL. Richard Heard. s/ Oct. 1,1817. p/ Jan. 5th, 1818. Wife Elizabeth. My four children: Daniel, Charles, Mary Heard and Elizabeth Norman. Granddaughter A. Caroline Norman. Wife Elizabeth, Daniel Heard and son-in-law Lewis Norman, exrs. Test. Willis Pope, John Coleman and John Roberson.

WILL. Jerome Miller. Nun-cupative. p/ Dec. 2nd, 1818. Ellinor King and Rachael Edwards swear they were present and heard Jerome Miller s a y on his dying bed that he had one bay mare, not mentioned in his d e e d of gift and that his wife should keep it during her life and after her death to be disposed of by a Trustee to furnish me a n d my wife a decent burial.

COURT RECORDS

Dec. 20, 1796. John Griffith of Wilkes County Ga. to James Hughey of Rutherford County, N. C., 287 1/2 acres in Franklin granted to said Griffith Aug. 31st, 1785. Test. Robert Griffith.

1796. Andrew Bell of Oglethorpe County, to John Hynds of Oglethorpe County, land on Oconee River, Jackson County, originally granted to Samuel Gardner 1786. Test Abel Gowen and Robert McCraney.

Aug. 30, 1795. Benjamin Stephens of Burke County to Mial J. Barnett of Franklin County, 287 1/2 acres near Cedar Shoals on Oconee River, originally granted to J o h n Wagnon in 1785. Test. John Barnett, J.P.

Feb. 7th, 1797. Samuel Gardner to John Cunningham, both of Jackson County. Test. Nathaniel Dean. Thomas Hightower.

June 26th, 1796. Benjamin Parr to John Barnett. Test. Wm. Hutchinson.

Jan. 28th, 1797. George McFall to John Cunningham. Bond to pay all damages arising from a n y claims to land conveyed by Samuel Gardner to said Cunningham, to lands on both sides of Cedar Creek, which deed was made July 6th, 1796. Test. James Pittman and Hugh Mains.

May 1st, 1796. William Lowe and wife, Fanny, of Lincoln County, to William Duke and Joseph Molton? of Jackson County, 690 acres on north fork Oconee River, Originally granted to John Gorham in 1787. Test. Phillip Zimmerman. Thos. Clark.

Dec. 10, 1796. Daniel Gunnells, exr. of Nicholas Gunnells, decd. to James Lindsey of Jackson County, 287 1/2 acres on north fork of Oconee River. Test. J. Moore.

Jan. 19th, 1797. Zachariah Lawrence of Oglethorpe County, to James Lindsey of Jackson County, 287 1/2 acres on north fork of Oconee River. Test. John Luckie.

Mar. 28th, 1795. John Rogers of Elbert County, to William Davis, ditto, 575 a. on Big Shoal Creek. Test. Wm. Chapman, Daniel White and Thos. B. Scott.

Dec. 21st, 1796. Thomas B. Scott, to Zachariah Collins, both of Elbert County, land on Oconee River, surveyed by Edward Collier. Test. Archelius Jarrett.

Aug. 13, 1795. James McCutchen of Elbert County to Joseph Shields of Oglethorpe County, 200 acres on Walnut fork. Granted to said McCutchen May 21st, 1790. Test. John King.

Aug. 17, 1797. Greene County Ga. Abraham Heard, Tax Collector, to William Phillips, R.P., given by John McCutchen, land on Cabin Creek, Jackson County. Test David Gresham and Peyton Smith.

May 22, 1797. Joseph Carson of Wilkes County, to Sampson Lane of Franklin Cty, land on Oconee River, Jackson County. Test. Joseph Dabb, John Lane, P. Williamson.

July 11, 1797. John Appling of Columbia County, to Thomas Screven of Jackson County, land on Trail Creek, north Oconee River, granted to Appling in 1786.

Mar. 16, 1795. Daniel Williams of Elbert County, to Purnal Truett of Wilkes County, land in Franklin County. Test. Allen Daniel and William Moss.

June 6, 1797. Briant Mooney, to Robt. Morgan, land on Sandy Creek, originally granted to said Mooney, Dec. 10th, 1788. Test. B. Harris. John Stiles.

Feb. 20, 1796. John King to Ruth Adair both of Franklin County, land on north fork of Oconee River. Test. Jacob Lindsey and Jacob Adair.

Nov. 28th, 1796. Micajah Williamson, Atty, at Law, of Wilkes County, to Wm. Hopkins of Jackson County, land on Greenbrier Creek, Jackson County. Test. John Barnett and John Dunn.

May 10, 1797. John H. Foster, to Danl. Price, both of Wilkes County, 287 1/2 acres in Franklin County, now Jackson County. Test. J. Derricott, R. Worsham.

May 20th, 1797. Daniel Price, T.C. of Wilkes County, to John H. Foster, land in Franklin County, 1,793 acres in arrears for taxes 1793. Test. J. Derricott and R. Worsham.

July 21, 1797. George Naylor, of Columbia County, to Alexander McLaws of Richmond County, a tract originally granted to Francis Gantall in 1795, sold for taxes. Test. Theodore Brightwell and John Appling.

July 7th, 1797. John Cobb of Jefferson County, to Alexander McLaws of Augusta, Richmond County, 287 1/2 acres in Franklin County, when surveyed on Mulberry fork, Oconee River. Test. Richard Lubbock and John Wilson.

Sep. 17th, 1796. William Strong, to Isham Strong, land on Big Creek, part of grant to Benjamin Ashworth. Test. William M. Stokes.

Feb. 15, 1797. Rebecca Puryear, Arthur Patton and Charles Dougherty, bond as adms. of the estate of Wm. Puryear, decd. late of this county. Test. James Armstrong

Oct. 1, 1796. John Appling of Columbia County, to William Heard, Jr, of Jackson County, land between north and middle fork of Oconee River.

Aug. 2, 1797. Robert Campbell, to John Raker? land on Oconee River, north fork, originally granted to Samuel Gardner. Test. R. Easley.

Nov. 28, 1796. John Rainey of Wilkes County, to Samuel Shields, of Oglethorpe County, land on both sides of Cedar Crk, Test. John Cunningham. Thomas Shields.

Dec. 10, 1796. Peter Strother and wife, Margaret, of Wilkes County, to Samuel Shields of Oglethorpe County, 287 1/2 acres on Cedar Creek, originally granted to William Mitchell 1785. Test. William Jones and Spencer Branham.

Oct. 10th, 1797. John Hart, Sheriff of Jackson County, to Russell Goodrich of Charleston S. C., land of Thomas Harwood, of State of Maryland. Several Surveys. (Harwood's wife, Anne White)

Oct. 4, 1796. Jonothan Jackson Hays, to John Phillip Hays, of Franklin County, ten dollars for land on Oconee River, Franklin County, now Jackson County. Originally surveyed and granted to Jenny Phillips, now the wife of said Hays. Test as above.

Oct. 10, 1797. Samuel Gardner of Jackson County, to Robert Bailey of Hancock County, land on Sandy Creek. Test. John Bailey and John Espy.

Dec. 2nd, 1790. William Hay, to David Hillhouse, both of Wilkes County, 500 a. south fork of Broad River, surveyed June 1794 for Wm. Hay. Test. Robert Creswell and D. Creswell.

March 11th, 1791. Richard Lockhart, of Greene County to David Criswell of Wilkes County, 287 1/2 acres on south fork of Broad River, Franklin County, now Jackson County. Test. James McFarland, Robert Creswell.

June 10th, 1796. John Hannah of Jackson County to Daniel Head of Elbert County, land on north fork of Oconee River. Test. William Head.

Aug. 23rd, 1791. Alexander Gordin?, to David Hillhouse, land partly in Wilkes and Elbert counties. Test. Edward Cowder. Isaac Heubert.

Apr. 11th, 1796. Daniel Price, Tax Collector of Wilkes County, to David Hillhouse, 3,400 acres in FRANKLIN County, land of Benjamin Allen, in arrears for taxes 1793. Test. R. Worsham.

Oct. 11, 1792. George McFalls to David Hillhouse, both of Wilkes County, 100 acres of land on Broad River, originally granted to said McFall 1791. Test. W. Hendley and B. Smith.

Mar. 12, 1792. David Hillhouse of Wilkes County to Thomas Hillhouse of New London County Connecticut, land in Franklin, Elbert and Wilkes County, being the same where my furnace and forge are located. Test. Wm. Boring and R. Worsham.

July 27th, 1896. Thomas Hillhouse of Montville Connecticut, to David Hillhouse of Wilkes County, above property. Test. James Murren and David Reed.

Mar. 27, 1797. David Hillhouse of Wilkes County, to William Longstreet of Augusta, Richmond County, one-fourth of above property. Test. John Hendley. B. Smith.

March 27th, 1797. David Hillhouse, to Buckner Harris, both of Wilkes County, one-fourth of the above. Test, as above.

Oct. 10th, 1797. William Deal and wife, Jemima, to Daniel W. Easley, land on north fork of Oconee River. Test. B. Easley and Paul Patrick.

WILL. James McGowan. (Oktibbeha Cty. Miss). s/ Sept. 27th, 1843. p/ Jan. 1844. Nephew James McGowan, spn of brother Samuel McGowan. Brother John McGowan. Children of my sister, Jane Shackleford. Brothers Edward and Hamilton McGowan. Nephew John Scott. Niece, Sophia Harden. Nephews John Harden and John and Thomas Ross. Exrs. brother Samuel McGowan. [The above approved by the testimony of Wm. Bell, Jacob Cobb and his wife, Missouri A. Cobb. Admitted to Probate Jackson County, January 1844.

WILL. Sherrod Thompson. s/ Sept. 16th, 1843. p/ same month. Sons: Jesse W., Wm. S., Green S. and Lewis D. Thompson. Daughter-in-law, Mourning Thompson, wife of Lewis, and her children. Daughter Caroline Bailey, wife of James Bailey, and her children. Sons: William S. and Green S. Exrs. Test. John J. McCullock, Samuel Watson and James H. Strange. Moses Potts.

WILL. William Lott. s/ Aug. 22, 1842. p/ Sept, 1843. Wife Jane. Two of my sons Moses and Enoch Lott and my other son, George Lott, to have one dollar. Moses and Enoch married. Brother George Lott. Test. Thomas Williams, Martha Bell and Washington Chambe?

WILL. George Hayes. s/ Jan. 25, 1841. p/ Nov. 1843. Wife Sarah. Son James E. Hayes. Daughter Mary, Lot No. 397, 12th, District Irwin County, "which I drew". To son Geo. B. Hayes and his wife. Son Thomas P.C. Hayes, daughter Srah and her children. Daughter Nancy. Daughter Rebecca. Daughter Sophia and her children. Daughter Betsy & her daughter Sarah Ann. Daughter Louisa & her children. Wife Sarah and friend Russell T. Jones, exrs. Test. Jackson Bell, E.H.Moomaugh? and Charles Witt.

WILL. William M. Adair. s/ Aug. 17,1844. p/ Sept. 1844. All estate to wife, Mary. James S. Orr, Exr. Test. Allen Justice and James M. Adair.

WILL. Henry Potts. s/ May 30th, 1847. p/ May 1849. "Old and infirm". Wife Unity.. If dtr. Elizabeth Caroline Potts outlives her mother, she to have control of my home, etc. Other children: Cicero Potts, Cynthia B. Pittman, Moses Potts & Hugh Potts. Wife Unity & dtr. Eliza C. Potts Exrs. Test. Thomas Stapler, A. D.Stapler & John J. Parks.

WILL. Mark Thornton. s/ Mar. 22, 1849. p/ May 7th, 1849. Wife Mary, life estate. All my property, "all my children". Wife Mary and son Stephen A. Thornton, exrs. Test. J.H.Cunningham. H.C.Giddens. S.R. Hood.

WILL. John T. Goodman. s/ Feb. 11, 1845 p/ Mar, 3, 1845. Wife Irena. sole heir & exr. Life estate to be divided between said wife and heirs at law, in case of marriage. Test. R.A.Oliver, H.C.Carter. M. A. Justice.

WILL. John Cash. s/ Oct. 7th, 1843. p/ January 1846. Daughter Bethany, wife of Samuel Strickland. Sons George B., Benjamin W., Joel P.? and his daughter Martha and her brothers and sisters, children of first wife. Daughter Polly, wife of Thos. McGuire. Daughter Nancy, wife of John Turk. Son Benjamin W. Cash and friend Noah H. Pittman, Exrs. Test. Archibald Moon and James H. Willis.

WILL. Robert Stapler. s/ Jan. 30, 1846, p/ May 2nd, 1846. Daughters Sarah M. and Mary H. Stapler. Daughter Armintha E. Rogers. Mentions two 40-acre lots drawn by him in the Cherokee purchase. Exrs. to have care of slave Abraham "left in my care by Ephraim Owens". Son-in-law Wm. S. Rogers, Exr. Test. Thomas Stapler, Saml. Smith, William G.Smith & Levi O. Tolbert.

WILL. Harrison Thurmond. s/ Oct. 22nd, 1843. p/ Mar. 2nd, 1846. Wife Jane B. and my 11 sons and four daughters, viz: James C., Thomas Jefferson; Harrison Montgomery, Geo, ? McIntire, Troup, Andrew Jackson, John Meredith. Christopher Columbus, Geo. Gilphin, Jesse Mercer, Anglin Anthony, Wm. Henry, Sarah Jane, Jenett Cinderella, Mandolin Octavia Thurmond and Mary Ann DeLaprierre. Mentions land in Tishomingo County Miss. given to James C. Thurmond. Mary Ann DeLaprierre to have her property in her onw right. Wife Jane B., son Wm. Henry, Exrs. and guardians. Test. Perry D. Braselton. Gustavus V. Braselton and Jacob Braselton.

WILL. Mary Smith. s/ Mar. 5th, 1846. p/ July 1846. "Old and infirm." Deed of gift to son Gideon Smith of all property to care for her. Test. W.M.Gatjright, Benajah Thornton.

WILL. Elizabeth Walker. s/ May 5, 1846, p/ July 1846. To friend and neighbor, Haden J. David, homeplace. To son Nathan, bed, etc, if he comes for it. To Wm. Vinson's children and Polly Street's children, clothes, etc. Son Augustus Walker, spinning wheel, etc.To Polly Ann Smith, plates, etc. Haden J. David, Exr. Test. Francis M. David. John Smith and W.M. Gathright.

WILL. William N. Lay. s/ Aug. 25, 1846. p/ Sept. 1846. Wife Winney. Sons: Marcus, John and Columbus. Daughters: Caroline, Ann, Mary and the unborn, as the become of age. George B. Wood and Wm. Lay, Exrs. Test. P.J.E.Griffith. George Thomey? and Richardson Lay.

WILL. Robert Ratchford. s/ June 15,1846 p/ Dec. 1st, 1846. Brother Joseph. To the children of my sister Polly Hawkins. Cousin William Henderson to stay on farm until brother Joseph takes charge. Polly's children, Franics Hope and Richard Baxter Hawkins. Test. Charles Dougherty, Sr. Charles Dougherty, Jr. Wm. Hannah.
(spelled Daugherty)

WILL. James Shankle. s/ Apr. 15, 1846. p/ March 1st, 1847. Wife Lucinda, minor children. Brother Seaborn M. Shankle. Wife Lucinda and brother Levi H. Shankle, Exrs. Test. Middleton Witt, James H. Hays and John H. Skinner.

WILL. Levi Lowry. s/ Jan. 29, 1847. p/ May 3, 1847. Wife Martha. To John J. McCullock, slaves. Granddaughter Sarah J. Lowry, under age. To grandson Camillus Few, a slave in trust for my daughter Martha W.Witt, now in possession of Chas. Witt. To grandson James Venable, son of John and Sarah Venable, in trust for the use of my daughter Sarah G. Venable and her children, several slaves. Sons John W. and Willis B. Lowry. To son Osborn M. Lowry, one dollar. Wife Martha, John J. McCullock and Willis B. Lowry, Exrs. Test Samuel Watson, Middleton Witt. John M. Skinner.
CODICIL. Mar. 12th, 1847. As guardian of the children of Leonidas Few., decd. bought house and lot in Covington Ga. for their use, which, if they refuse to receive, that the property devised to Camillus Few be given to John J. McCullock, James Venable and John W.F.Lowry.

WILL. William Langford. s/ Dec. 28,1840 p/ July 5,1847. "My wife" After her death all property to be divided between my step-son, Allen Langford and my own children, Elizabeth Crawford, Sarah Jane Wilson, Willis J. and Chatten L. Langford, Wife and Allen Langford, Exrs. Test. Ephraim Jackson, Wm. S. Smith, John Hartley.

WILL. Frederick Harvel. s/ Mar. 1, 1847 p/ July 5, 1847. Wife Letty. Nephew Frederick Harvel, Jr. Nephew Watson Harvel, $10.00. Other property to be divided between the above named Frederick Harvel, Oliver Harvel, Richard Harvel, William Harvel, Henry Harvel, Harriett Harvel. Frederick Harvel Jr. and Alfred Brooks, Exrs. Test. J.H.Cunningham and William M. Winters.

WILL. John Harrison. s/ Dec. 20, 1843. p/ Sept. 6th, 1847. "My wife", children, Daughters Ann, Sebby?, Mary, Caroline J., Sarah J., Margaret, Jane and son Thomas S. Harrison. Wife and son William P. Harrison, Exrs. Test. Wm. L. Mitchell, Saml. L. Watson and Robt. J. Millican.

WILL. Solomon Sexon. s/ July 22, 1845. p/ Jan. 10, 1847. "Far advanced in years" Wife, Susan, everything, having given his children all he could afford. Friend John Wofford, Exrs. Test. Jos. Davis, Moses Wofford and Absolom Wofford.

COURT OF ORDINARY Sept. term 1808? (shown as 1838, probably wrong)

Peter E. McMillan said he saw Horatio Webb inscribe as a witness to the will of Major James Cochran in which he divided his property between his wife, Mary Cochran, Judith Winn, Ann Key and Jane Thurmond. If there were other bequests it was some small amount to Jesse Horton, he was not sure there was anything. This was about ten years ago, as well as he could remember that James Cochran was of sound and disposing mind, etc. Horatio Webb, Andrew McClain and Jacob Braselton also testified to this. Jacob said he saw the will in 1833. (Peter E.McMillan-above)

July 4, 1808. Bolar Moon obtained letters of adm. on the estate of Jesse Moon, and Nancy Leon, on the estate of Andrew Leon.

MISCELLANEOUS RECORDS JACKSON COUNTY GEORGIA

September 5, 1808. William Wood obtains letters of adm. on estate of John Gregg, late of this county, deceased.

Last will of James Beard, produced and proven by Claborn Castleberry a n d James Barr. [Should be Jane or Jean Beard]

On petition of M a r y Jones, admtx. of J a m e s Jones, Decd., Benjamin Campbell made joint administrator.

Petition of Agrippa Atkinson that Sarah Durbin, admtx. of Luke Durbin, decd., makes clear title to a certain tract of land on Beech Creek. Granted.

Nov. 7th, 1808. William Wates obtains letters of adm. on estate of Volentine Hollingsworth, late of this county, decd.

Last will of David Dickson produced and proven by Alexa and Sarah Gillespie.

Statement of Jas. Shields, one of adm. of the estate of Patrick Shields, that there are four orphans and four small Negroes who will suffer for pork unless provision is made. Granted.

John Hanson, attorney for adm. of Thos. Rogers, claims Hugh Montgomery and Samuel Gardner have failed to qualify as guardians to the orphans of the s a i d decd., and asking that they be required to report at next court.

Ordered that Sally Turner, orphan of Butler Turner, be bound to David Witt, Esquire. She being about four years old. Carry Turner, d i t t o, bound to William Bardford. Carry about nine years old.

Henry Beart, an orphan about nine years old. His father, Henry Beart, not being a fit person to care for him, bound to Elijah Cowan, Esquire.

Jan. 2, 1809. William Shockley obtained letters of adm. on estate of Forgey Coven (Covee?), late of this county, decd.

Jacob Pettijohn obtains letters of adm. on the estate of Mary Slaton, will annexed, late of this county, decd. (Will not on record).

Ridley a n d Matthew McCullars, orphans of D a v i d McCullars, decd. choose Levi Lowry, Esquire, guardian.

Petition of Agrippi Atkinson, one of the securities for Mary Jones, admx. of James Jones, to be relieved because said Mary is about to move out of the county. She is ordered to appear at next Court.

On motion of Mr. Hanson that the wish of Thomas Rogers, decd. in his lifetime as stated to his brother Peleg Rogers, that his son Thomas Stanfer Rogers, now an orphan, be taught the science of law. Walton Harris agrees to take him till he is 21, if the estate allows him clothes, etc. Granted.

Petition of Martin Cleck a n d Malachi Cleck that t he adms. of Michael Borders of Elbert County, give clear title to 25 acres where said Cleck then lived, lying in the territory southwest of River Ohio in Greene County. Consideration of 400 pounds Virginia money. Jan. 2, 1809, Bond for title made Sept. 23rd, 1794 in Elbert County. Test. James Graham, Sr. and Jas. Graham, Jr.

B o n d assigned to Samuel Henderson by Holman Freeman Aug. 24, 1813.

Mar. 7, 1814. David Witt, Charles Venable and Samuel Henderson, Esquires: Hannah Henderson and Phenial Wilson obtained letters of adm. on the estate of James Henderson, Decd.

Russell J o n e s and John Espy obtains letters of adm. on the estate of Garrett W. Park, DECD.

Dixon Tillman, exr. estate of Nathaniel Trout, makes returns.

May, 2, 1814. Present: David Witt, Chas. Venable, Joseph Davis, Hosea Camp, Samuel Henderson: Sally Parker obtained letters of adm. on estate of Matthew W. Parker, deceased.

William Hancock obtained letters of adm. on the estate of John Hancock, decd.

Nancy Blackwell obtains letters of adm. on estate of Ambrose Blackwell, decd.

Receipt of N. Long to Phillip Thurmond, endorser of Thomas Morgan, for land in Baldwin County July 18, 1808.

May 1, 1809. Penny Farrow obtains ltrs. of adm. on estate of Perrin Farrow.

Last will of Nicholas Hobson produced and proven by James Rogers and David Tulley.

Last will of Nicholas Hobson produced and proven and letters granted. Test. John, Matthew and Baker Hobson.

Elizabeth Kirklin, admx. of William Kirklin, deceased, makes returns.

Mark Pulson, about 13 years old, bound to Samuel Watson.

Jane and James Shields, adms. of Patrick Shields, makes returns.

Thomas Ewing retired as Security for Isaac Cowan, as guardian of orphans of James Knox, decd. David Witt taking his place.

Jesse Mitchell prays that good titles be given to a certain tract of land in Oglethorpe County which William Ramsey, Sr. and Henry Ramsey gave bond for title in 1802; said Henry having since died, and John Pennington and Elizabeth Ramsey, adms., Elizabeth having since married Adair Pool.

Perrin Farrow gives bond for title to Adair Pool, lot No. 104, 25th, District Wilkinson County, Jan. 20th, 1808. Test. Thomas Watson, Taylor Duke. Ordered that the admx. of Perrin Farrow's estate make good titles.

Duncan Campbell of Jackson County, gave bond for title to one draw of land in contemplated land lottery, to John Hobson Aug. 1, 1806. He drew lot No. 170 in the 9th, District of Baldwin County. John assigned this land to Matthew Hobson, who prays that clear titles be given.

Samuel Hay and Priscilla Morgan qualified as Exrs. to the last will of William Morgan.

By his attorney, N. Harris, James Hendricks, Esquire, prays to be released as security for adm. of William Deal.

George N. Lyles, adm. of Leonard Marbury, prays to be dismissed.

In his lifetime William Deal of Jackson County sold land to Moses Herrin of Oglethorpe County. Moses asks for clear title.

July 3, 1809/ Abraham Chandler obtains letters of adm. pm estate of Bailey Chandler.

Harmon Holt obtains letters of adm. on the estate of Arthur Foster.

David Files and Joseph Davis obtains letters of adm. on estate of James Vann.

Last will of Phillip Aubury(Avery?), proven by James Hambleton and Johnson Frost?

James Rogers and Jonothan Lane pray to be released from the security of Daniel Johnson and Peleg Rogers adms. of Thomas Rogers, deceased.

EARLY COURT RECORDS

Aug. 27, 1796. John Ogletree of Wilkes County, to William McCree of Mecklenberg County, N.C., and Benjamin McCree of Oglethorpe County, 400 acres of south fork of Broad River in Franklin County, granted to Ogletree in 1794. Test. John Lee.

Feb. 10, 1798. Thomas Findley of Greene County to Elijah Hopkins of Jackson Cty., land on Greenbrier Creek. Test. Samuel Hopkins, Allen Harper. Joseph Claxton.

Dec. 14th, 1798. Thomas Wooten, Jr. to John Smith[red hair] 115 acres on Potters Creek. Test. Samuel Shields, Josiah Shields and Thomas Wooten.

Oct. 10th, 1797. Samuel Gardner to John Espy, land on Sandy Creek, adjacent land where said Epsy lives, 110 acres for $40, being part of 1,000 acres surveyed for & granted to Susannah Gardner, and conveyed to Samuel Gardner. Test. Isaac Hill. Jos. Embry.

June 7, 1796. State of Georgia. Greene County. Benjamin Watts to Henry Walker, both of above county, land on Walnut Crk. Test, E. Park and Thos. Carlton.

Jan. 2, 1797. Joseph McCutchen of Jackson County, to Henry Walker of Greene County, part of a grant of 600 acres, granted 1785, middle fork on Oconee River. Test. John King. Thos. Kirkpatrick.

Oct. 10th, 1798. John Scott and wife, Elizabeth of Jefferson County, to Ephraim Lindsey, late of Abbeville County, S. C., 500 acres granted Aug. 1, 1785. Test. John Coleman and Horatio Marbury.

Feb. 24th, 1799. William Strong, Sr. to John Moss, land adjacent to the land belonging to the heirs of Isham Strong, deceased. Test. Wm. Strong.

Nov. 28, 1798. Thomas Roberts of Chatham County Ga. to Jasper Johnson of Oglethorpe County, 575 acres on middle fork of Oconee River. Test. Talbot Arthur and Patton Weir.

April 12th, 1798. John Appling and wife Eleanor, of Columbia County, to Francis Loyall of Wilkes County, land on Oconee River, Jackson County, granted to John Appling 1786. Test. J. Perriman. Jeremiah Perriman and Paul Patrick.

Apr. 12th, 1799. Abraham Jones of Richmond County, to Eldridge Hargrove of Jefferson County, 500 acres on Mulberry fork originally surveyed for John Turner 1786. Test. James Bickley. N.H. Bugg.

Oct. 9, 1797. Receipt of William Carter for pay for slaves sold to Wm. Strong, Jr. Test. Joseph Norton. William Rousseau.

Nov. 15, 1797. William Milton and wife, Lucy, of Greene County, to Solomon Burford of Oglethorpe County, land on Rows Creek. Test. William Taylor. Thos. Tindley.

May 23, 1797. William Milton and wife, Lucy, and Daniel Williams and wife, Polly all of Greene County, to Mitchell and Solomon Burford, of Oglethorpe County, part of original grant to Micajah Williamson in 1787, on the Greene County line on Rows Creek in the Reserve Fort conveyed by Williamson to John Swepson? from him to Zachariah Cox; from him to George Taylor; from him to William Milton and from him to William Daniel. Signed William Milton, Lucy x Milton, William Daniel, Mary Kemp Daniel. Test. J. King, Thomas Smedley. Registered in Greene Cty. Sept. 16, 1798. Book G.

May 10, 1799. Benjamin Easley of Jackson County, to Robert Jackson of Washington County, land on Hurricane Shoals, Oconee River. Test. E. Hargrove. John Shields

May 10, 1799. Roderick Easley of Jackson County, to Robert Jackson of Washington County, land on Marbury's Creek and McMull ? and Barber's Creek. Test, E. Hargrove and John Shields,

May 2, 1797. James R. Whitney, T.C. of FRANKLIN, County, to John Blasingame of Greenville County, S. C., 287 1/2 acres surveyed for Benjamin Dooley 1785. Test. Polly Whitney and Moses Payne.
(same as above, same parties, surveyed in the name of Elias Mowers?)

Feb. 18, 1798. David Terrell of Wilkes County, to Thomas Rogers of Jackson Cty., 287 1/2 acres on Turkey Creek, originally granted to William Waggoner in 1795. Test. Will Terrell and Leidwell B. Montcastle.
(same dates, same parties, lands, surveyed in name of John Rench 1784. Test. John R. Whitney).

Dec. 7, 1797. John Thurmond to William Thurmond, both of Wilkes County, 100 a. on Oconee River, originally granted to Thos. Wooten in 1786. Test. Absolom Thurmond and Charles Thurmond.

Feb. 10, 1798. Thomas Findley of Greene County, to Samuel Hopkins of Jackson Cty. land on Greenbrier Creek.

1798. Jesse Willingham a n d his wife, Fanny, to John Weir, Sr., both of Oglethorpe County, land granted to Uriah Hardman in 1798. Test. William Ramsey, John Weir.

Sept. 6, 1798. William Head, Jr., planter, to George Ray, land between north and middle fork Oconee River. Test., Solomon Ray.

April 11th, 1799. John Hancock of Edgefield County S. C., to Benjamin Rogers of Jackson County, 287 1/2 acres in Jackson County. Test. Wm. H. Jack. John Cutliff.

WILL. William Matthews. s/ Sept. 16th, 1854. p/ Aug. 6th, 1855. "Knowing that I cannot live long according to the course of nature". Old Negro, Aggy, to live with her old mistress, or any child or grandchild s h e chooses. [only reference to wife.]. Son, Milton. Daughters: Elizabeth wife of John Creighton. Mary Matthews, Nancy and Mary Benton. Grandchildren, Wm., James and Martha Matthews, children of son Phineas Matthews, decd. Grandchildren Benjamin Franklin Matthews, Nancy Chandler, Polly Cain and Margaret Wade, children of son, Allen Matthews, decd. Son Milton Matthews, son-in-law John Creighton and John Benton, Exrs. Test. Thomas Stapler, Sr., Thomas Stapler, John M. Stapler and William T. Sharp.

WILL. Andrew H. Henderson. s/ Dec. 31, 1852. p/ Jan. 26, 1853. Wife Flora Olivia Henderson, several children - "my family" Son, William Benton Henderson to assist wife Flora as Extrx. when he arrives at age 21. Brother J o h n D. Henderson of Jackson County, Exr. Probated Hillsborough County Florida, true copy of will above. Test. G. Sisby?. Benjamin Hagler and E. A. Ramsey.

WILL. Elizabeth Flournoy. s/ Aug. 4th, 1855. p. October 1st, 1855. Daughter Mary Christiana, wife of James Venable, sole heir, James Venable, Exr. Test. John A. Millican, James Morris, Saml Venable.

WILL. Nathaniel Shotwell. s/ Jan. 3rd, 1842. p/ Dec. 3, 1855. "Being old". Wife Rebecca. To son Jesse Shotwell $10.00. To daughter Eleanor Koker, slave. Son-in-law John L. Williamson, a slave. To wife Rebecca, all other property, real and perspnal, at her death, to go to son-in-law J o h n L. Williamson, he to take care of her as long as she lives. Son-in-law John L. Williamson and wife, Rebecca Shotwell, Exrs. Test. Anderson Orr, Henry Merck and B. H. Oglesby.

WILL. Uriah Slaton. s/ Aug. 29th, 1853. p/ Jan. 1, 1856. "Knowing I must shortly depart this life". Wife M a r y. 'at her death, to be divided amongst my children' Friend, Robert White, Exr. Test. James O. T. Johnson, D. T. Camp and John Flanagan.

WILL. Hannah Craft. s/ Sept. 5th, 1855. p/ Feb. 4th, 1856. All property to sister Rebecca Craft as long as she lives. At her death, to go to brother Daniel Craft's daughter, Hannah, and sister Pegg's Mary. Two slaves to be sold for the support of Testatrix's sister, Martha, if s h e is still alive. Rebecca Craft, exr. Test. Henry Duke, Joel Johnson, B. F. Brown.

WILL. John Minnish. s/ Jan .22nd, 1856. p/ Apr. 7th, 1856. Everything to wife for the benefit of herself and support of the following children: Elizabeth Frances, M a r y Ann, Sidney Marssa?, John Wiley, Richard K i n g, Franklin Harrison. Wife Sidney and James E. Haggard, exrs. Test. James Lowe, James A. Brock, H. B. Gober.

WILL. Joseph A. Hughey. (Clarke Cty.) s/ July 17th, 1851. p/ June 2, 1856. Wife Susan. Daughter Susan Frances, wife of Edmond G. Elder. Daughter Mary Ann, son John Thomas. Daughter Elizabeth Caroline. Daughter Elizabeth Cloud. Son David Anderson. Son Joseph Barton Thrasher. Wife Susan, son John Thomas Hughey and son-law Edward G. Elder, exrs. Test. Thomas Booth, Thomas Simonton & John Calvin Johnson.

WILL. Milton B. Wood. Nun-cupative. p/ Aug. 9, 1856. Wife Frances, land recently purchased in Thomas County, etc., to be sold and money put at interest until the youngest child comes of age, then to be divided between wife, Frances, and "my children." Father, James Wood, Exr. Witnesses Homer R. Howard, Wm. M. Wood, Jas. M. Tait.

WILL. William M. Wood. Nun-cupative. Died Sept. 9th, 1856. His wife Elizabeth, to remain on the farm until the youngest child becomes of age. Son William to have the farm and take care of his mother until he becomes of age. When the division comes, the rest of the children to be m a d e equal with him. His father, James Wood, to see that his wishes are carried out. Witness John R. Hancock, William M. Duke and E. Whitehead.

WILL. James Hargrove. p/ Feb. 14, 185-? p/ Mar. 2, 1857. "Being old." Wife Elizabeth, all property her natural life. To Polly Prickett's nine children. Daughter Cynthia Gober. Son Asbury Hargrove. Son James P. Hargrove. Son William F. Hargrove. Daughter Hester Ann Butler's two children, James L. and Sarah Ann Butler. To daughter Nancy M. Butler, slave and a home with her mother as long she (Nancy) is a widow. Sons John W. and Seaborn Hargrove. To son Henry L. Hargrove, a home with his mother during her natural life. If she dies first, $1,000 to be put at interest so he may be well treated.. Not stinted as to clothes or diet. Step-daughter R. Hudson. Methodist church $50.00. Sons: Asbury, John W. and Seaborn G. Hargroves. Exrs. Test. W.B.J.Hardman, John M. Prickett and Seaborn M. Shankle.

WILL. Josiah L. Blalock. s/ Jan. 11th, 1857. p/ Apr. 6th, 1857. Wife Susan, life estate, all property to go to my children at her death. Daughters, Mary Catherine a n d Margaret Jane. Gold watch to Calvin J. Blalock, to be held in trust by my brother William H. Blalock until Calvin is of age. Robert Moon and Wm. H. Blalock Exrs. Test. Henry Hosch, E. Wilder, R.J. Park.

WILL. Noah C. Sharp. s/ Mar. 16, 1857. p/ May 4, 1857. All estate to sister Mary Evelyn S h a r p, who has nursed him thru much affliction. Also his interest in his father's estate, when divided. Mary E. Sharp, Extrx. Test. Thomas Stapler, Sr. William T. Murray, Lewis Sharp.

WILL. Isaac Borders. s/ Mar. 22, 1853. p/ July 6th, 1857. Sons: John H., Michael A. and Enoch H. Daughters: Polly Thornton Lucinda,wife of William Bowden? and her children.Matilda wife of Genl. Butler and her children. A n n , wife of William L. Wilbanks, and her children,decd. daughter Malinda Howard, whose children, Jesse, John a n d Virgil are minors. Test. Giles Mitchell, W.B.J.Hardman, C.W.Wood.

WILL. Middleton Brooks. s/ Nov. 3, 1848 p/ Dec. 1851. "Of advanced age", Daughter Betsy Kendrick. Granddaughter Forsytha Johnson Kendrick. Son Thomas a n d his children. Daughter Elizabeth, wife of Wm. Mangum. Son Alfred. Son Middleton. Daughter Malinda, wife of Aaron Kemp. Daughter Lavina Mangum. Daughter Rachael Mayo. Son Jarrett D. Brooks. Exr. Son, Alfred. Test. Mina Lipscomb, David P. Lipscomb. John J. McCullock.

WILL. David Holmes. s/ Oct. 15th, 1849. p/ Feb. 3rd, 1852. Wife Sarah. Legacy to surviving children of my daughter, Lucy Cunningham, one residing in Gwinnett Cty. The r e s t in Tennessee. After deducting the amount of a note on James Cunningham, to son John Holmes. Vivian Holmes, a legacy in trust for son Washington a n d his children, while he is so intemperate. Son Alexander Holmes. Son Henry Holmes. Daughter Caroline Harrard Holmes. Exr. G.L. G. Harris. Test. William Frost. Samuel Frost. John Kirkpatrick, John Reynolds.
(Sarah probably a secpnd wife as all slaves, etc. returned to her. Marriage contract mentions not to set up a claim to each other's property)

WILL. Joseph Davis. s/ Apr. 12th, 1852. p/ June 1852. Son Joseph H., daughters, plantation whereon I now live, take care of their mother. Daughters Louise Appleby, Elizabeth Webb, Elvira Hammond. Library of books divided among four sons. Those of children not named have received their share already. At the death of my wife, the property I give her, to be divided among her six children. Exrs. Sons Thomas J. and Joseph H. and son-in-law H.C. Appleby. Test. Wm. Henderson, N.H. Pendergrass and James Wofford.

WILL. Martha Lowry. s/ Nov. 29th, 1849. p/ July 5th, 1852. To John J. McCullock, slaves, etc. in trust for the use of my daughter, Mary E. McCullock and her children. He appointed Exr. also. Test. H.J. Randolph and Jos. F. Harrison.

WILL. Mary Cunningham. s/ Oct. 5, 1850. p/ Dec. 5, 1852. "Old and infirm" To sons John H. and Wm. J. Cunningham, all property, provided they give my son Ansel Cunningham's children $1,200. Said sons, Exrs. Test. P.P. Casey. A.J. Winters and S.A. Thornton.

WILL. John Rogers. s/ Dec. 4, 1852. p/ 6, 1853. Wife Sarah. Three sons: John Wm., James Thomas and Franklin Jackson Rogers to be educated out of the estate. Anything left, to be divided with my three eldest children: Elizabeth C. Thornton, Wm. S. Rogers and Sarah J. Potts. They having received their share. Exrs. wife, Sarah and friend Thomas Stapler. Test. Thomas Stapler, John M. Stapler, Carless A. Strickland, W. J. Pittman, John G. Strickland.

WILL. Elijah Lay. s/ May 10th, 1851. p/ Dec. 5th, 1853. "Of adavcned age". Wife, Martha, plantation, etc. At her death to go to Lourena Wood and Richardson Lay: Children of Wm. N. Lay, Mary C. McElhannon, Sarah Ann McElhannon. Heirs of David Lay, decd. viz: Samuel N. Lay, Mary E. Johnson, Larkin R. Lay, Elijah W. Lay, and Martha L. Lay, one dollar. Minors of Frances McElhannon, decd., Hezekiah McElhannon to keep their share until they come of age. Minors of son Wm. N. Lay, decd. Hugh McElhannon to keep their share until they come of age. Exrs. Richardson Lay and Hugh McElhannon. Test. Bailey Chandler, Zeno Perkins, J.C. Johnson.

WILL. Thomas C. Barron. s/ Jan. 11th, 1853. p/ Jan. 9, 1854. "Feeble in body". Son William Barron. Daughters Amanda Park and Elizabeth Ledbetter and Nancy Antionette Barron. Son Calvin Barron. Son W. Barron, Exrs. Test. William H. Mapkin, A. J. Williamson, Calvin H. Barron.

WILL. James Wheeler. s/ May 29th, 1849. p/ Mar. 6, 1854. "Old and infirm". To son John Wheeler's children, land on which John lives. To son Daniel, land whereon I now live. Daughter Charity Wheeler. Balance to be divided among all my children, except Daniel. Exrs. Son Daniel Wheeler. Test. J. H. Cunningham. J.P. Williamson, James H. Barr.

WILL. Absolom Crisler. s/ Mar. 14, 1853. p/ Apr. 3, 1854. "Of advanced age". Wife Anna, with whom I have lived 50 odd years Children of deceased son Joel S. Crisler, minors. Minor children of deceased daughter, Rosanna Dunson. Exrs. son Jeptha S. Crisler and friend H.A. Bennett. Test. E.D. Garborough, Seaborn M. Shankle & W. M. Hunter.

WILL. William D. Martin. s/ May 7, 1853 p/ April 1854. To Trustees of Jefferson Academy, 150 shares of R. R. and bank syock. To giles Mitchell and John J. McCullock, for the Methodist church, ditto, 40 shares. Friend Shadrack Hogan and his, daughter, Amanda Hogan. Friend Giles Mitchell. Friend James F. Pittman. Friend John S. Williamson. Friend Wm. Watson, son of my friend Samuel Watson. Legacies of $25.00 each to friends, Middleton Witt, Samuel Watson, etc. Test. P.F. Hinton, H. J. Randolph and J.G. McLester.

MISCELLANEOUS RECORDS JACKSON COUNTY GEORGIA

WILL. Margaret Nash. s/ Dec. 5th, 1850. p/ July 5, 1854. Heirs of Manor Stovall, my daughter deceased. Daughter Nancy, Daughter Hannah. Daughter Mary. Grandson Reuben S. Nash. Exrs/ Gabriel Nash. Test. Walton Harris, Martha Jane Nash and W.M. Gathright.

WILL. Elijah Oliver. s/ Jan. 7th, 1852. p/ June 5, 1854. To wife Mary, $500.00 in trust of Joshua H. Randolph. Four dtrs. Susnnah Bradley, Elizabeth Randolph, Sarah Miller & Nancy Randolph. To friend Joshua H. Randolph, Trustee of granddaughter, Mary Ann Caroline Horton, now Wood Exrs. friends Thomas Bradley, Wood L. Randolph, Wm. P. Miller, Joshua Reynolds. Test. P. F. Hinton. W.S.Thompson and J.C. Harrison.

WILL. Thomas Wills. s/ May 1, 1854. p/ Aug. 1, 1854. Wife Sarah. Children: Jas., Sary Ann, Willis Leander T.,Elizabeth, Martha, Cicero, Joseph and Martin Wills, all unmarried. Exrs. Wife Sarah, son Jas. E. and Leander T. Wills. Test. Stewart McElhannon,James R. McCleskey, Abner Wills

WILL. James Henderson. s/ Sep. 23, 1854 p/ Nov. 6, 1854.[planter]. Wife Clementia property during her life or widowhood until all children come of age. The Tennessee land between Andrew H. Henderson and myself, to be divided lengthwise and appraised accordingly. Exrs. Wife Clementia and son Thomas J. Henderson. Test. James Blackwell, J o h n R. Willis and Bennett Rylie.

WILL. John D. Dalton. s/ Sept. 21, 1854 p/ Dec. 4th, 1854. Wife Sarah, lived with her 44 years in strictest quiet. Three children still at home, daughter Jane Montgomery's part, wife of James M. Montgomery, and all her children, free from the disposition of her present or future husband. Ditto for daughter Nancy Dillport. Ditto for daughter Munasa Slayton, wife of Wm. Slayton, all three daughters legacy to be in trust of their brother, Vinstron? Dalton. Test. James McMillan - Russell J. Park, John Lancaster.

WILL. Michael Wilson. s/ Oct. 30, 1854. p/ Jan. 8th, 1855. "Advanced in years". Wife Susannah. Home place to four sons, Isaiah, Henry W., William Q. and Michael M. Wilson, after the death of my wife, Susannah. Two sons, John S. and Fennel S. Wilson, my land in Laurens County. To daughters, Rhody, Mary and Jane, one sow and bee hive each. To my daughter Dicey, one sheep. The pension I am applying for now the right of my father, if received after my death, to be equally divided. Exrs. Sons, John S., Isaiah and Michael M. Wilson. Test. Thomas Bennett, P.F.Hinton and J.W.Hargrove.

WILL. Benjamin Riden. s/ Jan. 16, 1852. p/ March 5th, 1855. "Of advanced age". To son Caleb D. Riden and William S. Rogers George W. Gray and Alfred Smith, my land I live on in Jackson County, joining M.A. Brooks, William Thurmond and Jackson Dixon, to be equally divided between them. To son, John S. Riden, $5.00. To son Elijah B. Riden, $5.00, to be paid them by above three men. Exr. son Caleb D. Riden. Test. Thomas S. Stapler, Linton C. Dunson and John Faraby.

WILL. Thomas Johnson. s/ Apr. 21, 1854. p/ Mar. 5th, 1855. "My wife" [not named]. son Josiah Johnson a n d daughter Jane Smith. Exr. Josiah Johnson. Test. John M. Matthews, Alfred Smith & John Creighton.

WILL. Edwin Pendergrass. s/ May 29th, 1855. p/ June 4, 1855. Wife Elizabeth and four children, heirs. Exr. Wm. J. Parks. Test. James R. McCleskey, John Seay, Sr., John Pendergrass.

WILL. Mary Stewart. s/ May 6, 1855. p/ Jult 2, 1855. Homeplace in trust of John A. Heard, for her two daughters, Sarah Ann and Elizabeth Catherine, for them and their heris forever. Other property to be divided in six equal parts and given to above two daughters, a n d son James Row, son William Elder. Grandson Griffin Marcellus,the sixth part to t he three children of my son Richard, to-wit: John Griffin, James Thomas and Mary Jane. Exr.

WILL, Mary Stewart - concluded
John A. Heard. Test. John J. Cheatham, James M. Varnum and Hawkins H. Wright.

WILL. Joseph T. Cunningham. s/ Aug. 13, 1848. p/ June 17th, 1849. Wife Agnes. Son Joseph Christopher. Son Hugh M. Son Andrew. Son Columbus G. Cunningham. Daughters, Jane E., Amanda and Margaret Liddle, wife of A. J. Liddle, Cynthia A. Story, Wlizebeth Hemphill, wife of Phillip W. Hemphill, and her three children, Esther Agnes, Cynthia Adeline and Mary Elizabeth Exrs. John H. Cunningham, Giles Mitchell, for all land, etc. in Georgia. Hugh M. Andrew and Columbus G. Cunningham to carry out the will in Alabama. CODICIL Alonzo G. Story, appt. in place of H.M.Cunningham, decd. Test. James Montgomery, Benjamin McKenzie, Samuel Pool, W.H.Williams. Special term, orphans Court, April 18th, 1849, Talladega Alabama. Probated April 18th, 1849.

WILL. Benjamin Stockton. s/ Mar. 16th, 1846. p/ May 7th, 1849. First wife Elizabeth Stockton, and to each of her children, one dollar and no more. To Elizabeth Lile, one dollar and no more. Present wife, Sarah Stockton; daughter Thirza Ann Stockton, son James, all property to be divided equally between James M. Stockton Margaret Gillman, Elizabeth Blair, Marthy Kidd, Sarah McDuffie Martin and Thirza Ann Stockton. Exrs. James M. Stockton and Thomas J.Kidd. Test. Joshua Wilson, Moses Brian and Perry Bowen.

WILL. William M. Winters. s/ Oct. 21st, 1850. p/ July 7, 1851. Wife Angelina, under bodily affliction and about to go south. Everything to be divided between her children at her death. Exrs. Wife, Angelina and friend James D. Henderson. Test. William Lyle, Thomas J. Bowen.

WILL. John Rogers. s/ May 15, 1849. p/ Sept. 1, 1851. "Of advanced age". Eldest son Jacob. Son Enoch. Daughters: Temperance Pettijohn, Sally Rudling, Nancy Poly and Permelia Rolling. James Pettijohn, husband of Temperance. Exrs. Sons Thomas and Jacob. Test. Ransom Seay, Jesse Windzor and James T. Rogers.

WILL. Jonothan Freeman. s/ Jan. 27th, 1851. p/ Mac. 5, 1852. Wife Mariah, property to be used for education of my five children. Daughter Elizabeth. Son James Martin. Daughter Edna. Daughter Sarah Angeline. Son John A. Benton. Wife Mariah and brother-in-law Edward G. Riley, exrs. Test. Thomas S. Stapler, George T. Pittman. Jefferson Thurnond. W.A.Brooks.

WILL. William Park. s/ Oct. 14th, 1851. p/ Dec. 3, 1851. Should Nancy Park, present wife, have a child, it to share with the others. Railroad stock set aside to educate the younger children. Grandsons James, William and John Wood, son of my daughter, Polly Wood. Daughters, Sally Giddens, Leury? Fowler and her sons Thos. and William, under age. Daughter Peggy Park. Daughter Jane Mitchell. Daughter Betsy Park. Daughter Emily Lester. Daughter Anna Parks. Sons Robert C., William and John Park. Exrs. Son Robert C. Son-in law Josiah Lester and son-in-law Jonothan Mitchell. Test. John Merck. Martin Graham and E.M.Johnson.

WILL. Nathan J. Sharp. s/ June 28, 1847 p/ Sept. 4, 1848. Wife Jane. Sons: Wm. T. Edmond J., Noah C., Carlos M., Russell H. and Jarrell G. Sharp. Daughters: Mary E and Marilla P. Sharp. If wife dies before all the children come of age, his brother Lewis J. Sharp to manage them. Exr. Lewis J.Sharp. Test. Thomas Stapler, William H. Stapler, George W. Gray and Sarah S. McElroy.

WILL. Solomon Kerbow. s/ Oct. 22, 1848. p/ Jan. 28, 1849. "Of advanced age". Wife Selah, with whom I have lived in the strictest of quiet for many years. Youngest son, Singleton Kerbow. Sons: Jesse M. Francis M. and John Kerbow. Wife Selah, son Jesse M. Exrs. Test. Robert Moon, Meredith Hutchins and John G. House.

WILL. Ludwell Worsham. s/ Mar. 19,1849. p/ Apr. 16,1849. Wife Nancy, at her death to be divided among my three daughters, viz: Frances M. Marler, Mary C. Moon and Elizabeth B. Thurmond. Sons: H. Worsham, Wynne A. Worsham. To Thomas J. Thurmond, the land he lives on. Sons John H. and Wynne A. Worsham, wife Nancy and son-in law Peterson T. Marler, Exrs. Test. Wm. Appleby, J.O.Pittman, Wm. Gathright.

WILL. Mary Anthony. s/ Jan. 20th, 1849. p/ May 7, 1849. "Old and infirm". Daughter Lucretia, her husband Thos. Lord and her son Ezekiel Anthony. Sons Wade and Thomas Anthony. All the rest of the property to be equally divided among my lawful heirs, except my son Willis Anthony, not to have any part of the land in Dooly County. Thomas and Wade Anthony, Exrs. Test. Martin Anthony, William Lord, James E. Haggard.

WILL. Henry C. Morris. s/ Mar. 16,1848. p/ March 14th, 1849. "My beloved wife," Everything to her to raise our children. William C. Hill and Henry Hosch, Exrs. Test. John Hays, Jonothan S. McClaine. Robert White.

WILL. Isaac Minnish. s/ Nov. 22, 1843. p/ July 2, 1849. "Old and infirm". Wife, Agnes. Daughter, Elizabeth Minnish, the survivor to dispose of the estate as she sees fit. Exr. James Hargrove. Test. Wade Anthony, James W. Shankle, Thomas Lord.

WILL. Joseph Landrum. s/ Dec. 24, 1842. p/ Sept. 3rd, 1849. Wife Sarah. To Elizabeth Landrum, wife of Jackson Landrum, decd. five dollars. After his decease, all property to be sold, and divided equally between son Jeptha and daughters, Sarah Ellison, Emily Davis, Elizabeth Bosworth, the heris of Prunella McElhannon, the heirs of Espy Lay and the heirs of my son, Larkin, decd. I allow Hugh McElhannon to keep the two shares for heirs of Prunella McElhannon and of Espy Lay, until they come of age; and Samuel Ellison to keep the share of the heirs of son Larkin, Decd., ditto, Hugh McElhannon.

Jeptha Landrum and Ezekiel Hewett, Exrs. Test. G. B. Wood, Hezekiah McElhannon and Hugh McElhannon.

WILL. James Welborn. s/ May 3, 1857. p/ Aug. 3, 1857. Wife Elizabeth. Sons James L. and John G. or /Y. Welborn and John Jasper Cook to remain on the farm & take care of their mother and sister, Hannah Welborn. To William Welborn's sons Cobb and Innes, land where William now lives. Land to Simeon, son of M.H.Welborn, land now in lititgation. To A.T.Welborn's sons, James C. and William. Exrs. James Welborn & B.F.Burson. Test. W.G.McElhannon, Carlson Steed and James Hoopaugh.

WILL. Middleton Witt. s/ June 21, 1853. p/ Aug. 1857. Wife Sarah A. To Miss? Martha J. Watson, his legacy from William D. Martin, Decd. Mentions his part of the estate of his father, David Witt, decd. To friend Dr. John M. Eskridge, $5,000. To friend N.H.Pendergrass, money. Esteemed friend Andrew M. Park, Exr. Caveat filed by Sarah A. Witt. Test. Jackson Bell, J.H.Randolph, J.G.McLester.

WILL. James Hodge. s/ Dec. 27, 1854. p/ Nov. 2, 1857. "Old and infirm". Wife Jenny. Daughter Nancy E. Hodge. Daughter Jenny M.,wife of Frederick Harwell and her children, said Frederick to have management of the property of my daughter, Zimley? Harwell's children until they are 21 Exr. son-in-law Frederick Harwell. Test. Wm. P. Miller. Willis Webb. B.F.Park.

WILL. Coleman Harrison. s/ Feb. 1,1857. p/ December 7, 1857. "Advanced in years", Wife Frances. Heirs of son Joseph Harrison. Son Jason C. Harrison. Sons-in-law Hilliard J. and Tandy K. Randolph. Son Thaddeus L. Harrison, Daughter Melisson Ann Hutchins. Daughter Sarah D. Brown. Exrs. Son-in-law Thomas A. Brown. Sons Jason C. and Thaddeus L. Hodge. Test. P. F. Hinton, J.E.Harrison. John W.Freeman.

WILL. Sterling Chandler. s/ 1855. p/ May 3, 1858. Wife Edith and all my children. Wife Edith and son Dudley J. Exrs. Test. Isaac M. David. Nathaniel Hicks and /Oliver Hobbs.

WILL. Sanford W. Johnson. s/ Apr. 2, 1858 p/ May 3rd, 1858. Wife Elizabeth and each one of my children to have one equal portion when they become of age. Wife Elizabeth, Extrx. Test. Archibald Moon, Floyd Benton and Phillip W. Moon.

WILL. William M. Gathright. s/ Oct. 2, 1852. p/ Aug. 3, 1858. Wife Milly. Daughter M i l l y Pittman, "who stayed longer with us than the others". Daughter Sally Pittman. Daughter Caroline Potts. Sons John C., William M. and Zebulon P. Gathright. Sons-in-law Wilkins Haynie and A. Pittman, Exrs. Test. Moses H. Potts, Delmas L. Jarrett. Thomas Stapler, William Appleby.

WILL. William Thurmond. s/ May 19, 1858... p/ Nov. 1858. Wife Permely, at her death, daughter M a r y and son Elisha Thurmond, who have no land, be made equal with the children who have. Exr. John Simpkins. William Lord, Sr. W.B.J. Hardman, Martha Thurmond.

WILL. Wood L. Randolph. s/ Apr. 18th, 1858. p/ Apr. 4th, 1859. Wife Elizabeth. Daughter Nancy F. Gilmore, wife of James Gilmore, trustee with John C. Randolph, for her son, Tillman Harrison Brown. Grandchildren Martha P. a n d Elijah W., children of my son, Elijah W. Randolph, to be in the hands of son, W.L.O. Randolph and son-in-law David P. Lipscomb. Daughters Mary E. and Mary Ann, unmarried. Sons Washington R. a n d Hilliard J. Randolph, be made equal with John C. a n d W.L.O. Randolph when of age. Extrx. Wife Elizabeth. Test. P.F. Hinton, T.J. Kidd, Christopher Kidd.

WILL. John C. Watkins. s/ Nov. 20, 1848. p/ Jan. 6th, 1859. Wife Jane. Son Luke T. Watkins, sole heirs and exrs. Test. Christopher Kidd, Thomas J. Kidd. Ramona? Marlow.

WILL. Elizabeth Minnish. s/ June 26th, 1855. p/ June 6, 1859. "Advanced in life" Niece Elizabeth Jane Minnish, sole legatee. James Hargrove and Levi H. Shankle, Exrs. Test. John F. Gober, Ezekiel Anthony, Levi G. Eubanks.

WILL. Hardy Howard. s/ Aug. 13th, 1859. p/ Sept. 12th, 1859. Sons: Samuel, Hartsford, Hardy a n d Homer R. Howard. Grandchildren Virgil John a n d Harper Howard, sons of Harper H. Howard. Daughter Emily Niblack, Amanda Webb. Daughter Elizabeth Webb and her two children, one a daughter of J.O. Webb. Daughter Malissa Braselton. Sons-in-law Hugh M. Niblack and Green M. Duke, exrs. Test. Ephraim Jackson, R.E. Oliver and N.H. Pendergrass.

WILL. James R. McCleskey. No date shown "Single man". That he a n d his brother J a m e s G. had agreed that whoever died first, survivor should have full control of property and continue to take care of the three sisters who lived with them, the two other sisters being well provided for. [died Nov. 26th, 1859]. Test. Henry Newton, John Venable, Jonothan B. S? Davis? and N.H. Pendergrass.

WILL. Charles Dougherty, Sr. s/ June 9, 1847. p/ Nov. 5, 1849. William F. Mann, an orphan boy, I have raised, under age, a slave. Rest to son Charles Dougherty, Jr. and son-in-law Andrew Oliver. Friend Middleton Witt, Esquire, my Exr. Test. J.H. Randolph, Henry R.J. Long, Giles Mitchell.

WILL. Elizabeth Strickland. s/ May 5, 1850. p/ May 6th, 1852. Caroline Story, wife of James F. Story, a n d her heirs, slaves a n d home whereon I lived before marriage with my present husband, be secured? & enjoyed during her life. After her death, equally divided between her heirs. To my husband, Hardy Strickland, a slave. It is my desire that my friend, Caroline Story, have my wearing apparel. Exrs. Giles Mitchell. Test. James Sissom John J. Sissom, Shadrack Hogan.

WILL. Lemuel Brown. s/ May 14th, 1842. p/ Sept. 6th, 1850. Wife Betsy, all real estate, both real and personal, consisting of a tract of land on which I now live, conveyed to me this day by my step spn, William S. Mitchell, life estate to her. At her death to go to my son, Thos. S. Brown. Should he die without children

WILL- Lemuel Brown - concluded
before his mother, the same to be vested in a Trustee for the use of my daughter Elizabeth C. Brooker and her children, free from the control of her husband, James Brooker. My deceased son, Samuel T. Brown, served in the army of Texas and fought for its independence, and by the laws of Texas, was entitled to a bounty of land, which will be mind. This to be divided between the two children already named. Son Thomas S. Brown, Exr. Test. Wm. S. Mitchell, Hugh Mitchell, James Langston, Coleman Harrison and T. M. Harrison.

WILL. James Booth. s/ Apr. 20th, 1845. p/ Nov. 4, 1850. Wife Sarah. Eldest son, John A. Booth. Second son, James Booth, both under age. Also younger children. Wife Sarah, Extrx. Test. John A. Booth, Brookfield Burson, James Alexander.

WILL. Fennel Hendrix. s/ Sept. 16th, 1850. p/ Nov. 4, 1850. Crop made between myself, my brothers, Thomas and James Hendrix, also with Moses Hendrix, brother Berry Hendrix; mother Sarah, and all that live with her. Brother Berry, Exr. Test. James Hargrove, William P. Carter, John W. Pruitt.

WILL. Joseph McLester. s/ Oct. 15, 1850. p/ Jan. 13, 1851. "Of advanced age". Wife Rhoda. Daughter Cynthia McLester. Daughter Caroline Judson McLester. To sons James G. and William McLester, my half of a town lot in Jefferson, whereon they are now doing business. Said two sons, Exrs. [Live with wife in peace and harmony 48 years]. Test. Benajah Thornton. J.H.Wade and Jeptha S. Crisler.

WILL. Robert M. Holliday. s/ Nov. 15th, 1850. p/ Jan. 13, 1851. Wife Mariah Dougherty Holliday. Sons Francis M. and Walton H. Holliday. Daughters, Beatrice M. and Julia C. Holliday. No/ exr. named. Test. Charles Witt, William Hunter, Elisha Martin. COFICIL. The land I am entitled to draw under the late Act of Congress of the U. S. for military services, be divided between Adolphus B. and Jeremiah R., Francis M. and Walton H. Holliday and Victoria M. Grant, vested in her lawful children. Nov. 30th, 1850. Test. Elisha Martin, James Martin, Charles Witt.

WILL. Polly Craft. [Clarke County]. s/ Nov. 17, 1846. p/ Mar. 5, 1860. Daughters Hannah and Rebecca Craft, sole heirs and Exrs. Test. Stephen Jackson. Samuel G. Locklin and Daniel Craft.

WILL. Jonothan Kolb. s/ Nov. 11, 1811. p/ Mar. 12th, 1812. Wife Susannah. First child, Harrison Kolb, the rest of my children which are, Nancy, Sophia, Rebecca, Harmon, James, Mary Ann, Jonothan, Rebecca J. and Susannah. Wife Susannah and James Cash, Exrs. Test. Ephraim Lindsey and Patrick Cash.

EARLY COURT RECORDS

April 3, 1798. Charles Dougherty, Sheriff, to Edward Callahan, his own lands, etc., sold to satisfy a judgement.

Oct. 14th, 1786. John Turner of Chatham County, to Abraham Jones, of Augusta, 575 acres in Franklin County. Test. Thomas Cummings and Benjamin Wall.

Sept. 1, 1799. James Wallace to Robert Flournoy, 287 1/2 a.granted to said Jas. Wallace in 1788. Test. John Marcus. Jos. Allison.

Nov. 26, 1789. William Pinson, to Robt. Flournoy of Greene County, 287 1/2 acres in Franklin County on the Oconee River. Granted Dec. 16, 1788. Test. John Marcus, Mary McFarland. Proved by John Marcus in Greene County Ga. 1789.

Oct. 23rd, 1799. Eldridge Hargrove and Roderick Easley, to George Smith, lot No. 14, in the town of Clarksborough, adjacent on the STH.by Broad Street. Test . B. Easley. Joseph McCutchen.

Dec. 6th, 1799. Jesse Lee of Oglethorpe County, to John Bradshaw of Jackson Cty. 200 acres on Currie's Creek, originally granted to Samuel Dickey. Test. Burwell Pope.

Jan. 19, 1800. Samuel Hopkins to Bethesda Hopkins, and her son Aaron Hopkins, all of Jackson County, $100.00 for 100 acres to Bethesda her lifetime and at her death, to her son Aaron Hopkins, land on Greenbrier Creek. Test. Robert McAlpin and Mary McAlpin.

Aug. 16, 1798. Col. William Milton, of Greene County, to Phillip Tignor, of Jackson County, 357 acres on Bear Creek, part of original grant to Micajah Williamson, whereon s a i d Phillip Tignor now lives. Test. John Beauchamp. Ster Nobles.

October 8, 1799. Joseph Cook of Greene County, to John Depriest of Jackson Cty., adm. of Shem Cook, decd., land on Walnut fork of Oconee River, being in the Continental Reserve, granted as bounty to Shem Cook May 24, 1784. Test. G.W.Foster, John Gilmer.

Oct. 7, 1798. Thomas Glascock of Richmond County, to William Matthews of Oglethorpe County, 287 1/2 acres in Franklin County, when surveyed for William Walker in 1785. Conveyed by him to Thomas Glascock in 1791. Test. Geo. Matthews Jr. and John Wilson.

Dec. 5th, 1795. John Fuller, a planter, to Thomas Glascock of Richmond County. Test. William Robertson.

Mar. 4, 1799. Sampson Lane of Franklin County to Anderson Watson of Jackson Cty. 225 acres on Oconee River. Test. William Rainey and Talbot Arthur.

May 18th, 1799. Receipt of Henry Carter for pay for slaves sold to William Strong Test. Ellis and A.B.Ogletree.

Sept. 3, 1799. Charles Dougherty, Sheriff, to William Milton of Greene County.

In court CHATHAM County Ga. John Holland received a judgement vs. Zachariah Cox. Land in Franklin County sold.

May 1st, 1798. John Boyd of Pendleton County S. C. to Elijah Wells of Jackson County Ga. land on Turkey Creek, former Franklin County. Test. Jacob Earnest and William Edmondson.

April 2nd, 1798. Ezekiel Wells, to Mark Thornton, 287 1/2 acres of land on Turkey Creek originally granted to Clement Stewart. Test. James Thurmond. Robert Burk.

Jan. 4th, 1799. Reuben Easten of Elbert County, to James Hitchcock of Oglethorpe County, 287 1/2 acres on Cedar Creek. Test. Wm. Davis. Nancy Davis.

Nov. 3, 1798. Micajah Benge, Thomas Bishop and Zebediah Briggs, all of Jackson County, land on the county line. Test Stephen Bishop, Josiah McDaniel, Robert McAlpin.

Aug. 4, 1799. Benjamin Rogers and wife, Unity, to Dempsey Rogers, land on Sandy Creek.. Test. Charles Sorrells, William Carter.

Apr. 30th, 1799. Peter Cobb, to Charles Gates, land on Crooked Creek. Test. James Martin and John Hampton.

Apr. 4, 1799. Charles Dougherty, Sheriff, to William Milton of Greene County, goods, etc. of George Naylor of Columbia County, including land in Jackson County. Test. John McFall. Joseph McCutchen.

Nov. 2nd, 1799. Thomas Patton, to John Patton, land on north fork of Oconee R. Signed M. Nall.

Mar. 25, 1800. Charles Dougherty, Sheriff, to John Barnett, goods, etc. of Edmund Hendley, adm. of John Gorham, decd., including land drawn by said John Gorham. Struck off to Edmund Hendley on his bid, released to John Barnett.Test. John McFall

Feb. 14,1800. Jasper Phillips pf Greene County, to Isaiah Goolsby of Oglethorpe County, 450 acres on Apalacha River and Goolsby's Creek. Test. E. Park. W.Patrick

Oct. 3rd, 1799. J. Hardin Foster, T.C. for Wilkes County, to William Gathright, land in Jackson County, on Sandy Creek, Oconee River, surveyed for William Young in 1785, in arrears for taxes to 1798.
/Test. R. Worsham.

June 12, 1798. Joel Bowen of Edgefield County, S. C. to Robert Wilson of Jackson County, Ga. land in Jackson County Ga. Test. Julius Nichols, Jr. John M. Moore, Abram Lindsey, Claborn Barnett. Sworn to In Jackson County 1800 by Abram Lindsey.

August 3, 1799. Robert Wilson to John Barnett, 287 1/2 acres on north fork of Oconee River, originally granted to Joel Bowen. Test. Robert Huddleston, James Pittman.

Feb. 26, 1800. Benjamin Porter of Wilkes County, attorney for Patrick Neal, to John Barnett of Jackson County, land on the Oconee River, granted to Patrick Neal, Nov. 30, 1784. Test. Thomas Napier and John Casey.

Mar. 24, 1800. Russell Jones of Oglethorpe County, to John Martin of Jackson County, 287 1/2 acres, originally granted to Samuel Gardner in 1787. Test. Wm. Strong.

June 29th, 1799. Joseph McCutchen to George Hays, 37 acres on Currie's Creek part of original grant to Peter Wiley, conveyed to him by said McCutchen. Test. Thomas Kirkpatrick.

Dec. 21st, 1799. Mary Gibson and Moses Hunt of Pendleton, S. C.(county) in Washington District, to George Hays of Jackson County, land on Currie's Creek, Jackson County. Test. Thomas Hays and Nancy Gibson.

Jan. 8th, 1800. John Cobb of Jefferson County, to William Hopkins, of Jackson County, 1,150 acres on Barber's Creek. Test. Jos. Clarkson & R. Easley.

April 30th, 1799. Valentine Gates to Charles Gates. Test. James Martin. John Hampton.

Mar. 23, 1800. Micajah Williamson and wife, Polly, to John Floyd, 280 acres on Greenbrier Creek, on which said John Floyd lives. Test. Jacob Carter.

Feb. 4, 1800. J o h n Rainey and wife, Ann, of Wilkes County, to Nathaniel Dean of Jackson County, land on Cedar Creek, part of the John Gorham tract granted in 1785. Test. Burkell Dean. Absolom Rainey

Aug. 2, 1799. William Rice, to son Benjamin Rice, deed of gift of slaves. Test. John Smith.

Dec. 27th, 1798. William Watkins, to Jacob Lindsey, land on north fork of Oconee River, originally granted to Isaac Fuller in 1798. Test. Abram Lindsey. Sally Upton

Nov. 5, 1797. Cordy Pate of Oglethorpe County, to Jacob Lindsey of Jackson Cty., land on Walnut Creek, part of an original survey to George McFall. Test.John, Abram and Josiah Lindsey.

Dec. 4th, 1794. James R. Whitney, T.C. for Franklin County, to John Cobb, 230 acres surveyed for Joseph Waller in 1784.

Aug. 15, 1799. Johnson Strong to Chas. Garner, land on Oconee River, the fishery Reserve. Test. William Stone, Robert Wilson and Noah Hutson.

May 21, 1800. Agreement. Edmond Taylor of Jackson County and George Weatherby of Jefferson County, that George Weatherby has received $400.00, sold t o Taylor 200 acres where James Cogburn now lives.Test. John McConnell, Thomas Bankston.

Feb. 24, 1800. John Templeton of Jackson County to Thomas McIntier of N.C. 300 acres on Oconee River for $50.00, originally granted to Templeton. Test. Susannah Wood. John McCartney.

Mar. 11th, 1799. Burwell Pope and wife, Priscilla, of Oglethorpe County, to Saml. Barnett of Greene County, 187 1/2 acres on north fork of Oconee River, originally granted to James Martin. Test, George Phillips and James Freeman.

Mar. 2, 1799. Solomon Strickland of Elbert County to John Patrick Jr. of Greene County, 125 acres on Shoal Creek, originally granted to Nathan Barnett in 1784.

Test. William Hutchinson. H. Strickland and John Strickland.

Mar. 1st, 1799. Arthur Patton, to John Billups, the land on Big Shoal Creek. Originally granted to T h o m a s Wooten in 1786. Test. Charles Dougherty, James McMillan and Jos. McCutchen.

Jan. 23, 1799. George Ray, planter, to Edward Phillips, planter, land on north fork of Oconee River. Test. Samuel Hathorn John Robison and Solomon Ray.

Nov. 16, 1798. George Sibbald of Augusta, Richmond County, power of attorney to Micajah Williamson, to sell, etc. all property in Jackson County. Test. J o h n Milton, Thomas P. Carnes.
[Given in Jefferson County, Georgia]

Feb. 22nd, 1799. James Tuttle to Thomas Banks, 28 acres on Cabin Creek. Test. James and David Little.

Feb. 4, 1799. Ezekiel Wells of Jackson County, to George Hall of Greene County, 287 1/2 acres on Mulberry fork, originally surveyed for John Garrett 1785. Test Samuel Gardner, Joseph Hines?

Nov. 15th, 1798. Micajah Williamson, to Micajah Benge, part of a tract granted to Micajah Williamson, Sr. in his lifetime. Test. John Marcus, John M. Carter.

Aug. 21, 1799. Thomas Patton to William Patton. Test. M. Nall.

Sept. 1800. William Rice, to son Jeremiah Rice, deed of gift of nine slaves. Test. M. Williamson, Robert Smith.

Oct. 1, 1799. Peter Williamson and wife Susannah, to John Foster, all of Greene County, land in Jackson County, originally granted to Micajah Williamson. Test. William Milton, Moses Speer. Benj Jepson.

Dec. 27th, 1798. James R. Whitney, T.C. of Franklin County, to Benjamin Echols of Franklin County, land originally granted to Brandrick Truce in 1785. Test. George Hemming, Henry Chapelier. Thomas Cruse and R. Walton.

Dec. 27, 1798. James R. Whitney, T.C. Franklin County, to Benjamin Echols of Franklin County, 230 acres, originally surveyed for Rowland Lankister 1785. Test George Hemming, Henry Chapelier. Thomas Cruse and Robert Walton.

Thomas Watson, guardian. The Court having appointed to said Thomas Ward, (Watson?), guardian for Thomas Ward, another orphan of said decd. Letters of guardian ship re-granted said Thos. Watson, etc.

July 4, 1814. Benjamin Fuller, Exr. of the estate of Thomas Bailey, late of Morgan County, in right of his wife, Mary, Fuller, former M a r y Bailey, produced a certified copy of the proceedings in Morgan County and asked it to be transferred to Jackson County. Granted.

Joseph Davis, David Dickson, James Tillman, Exrs. of the estate of John Wright deceased, granted permission sell certain tracts of land.

William Potts chosen guardian to Harmon Kolb, orphan of Jonothan Kolb.

J o h n Borders makes returns for four years on the estate of Michael Borders, deceased.

August 1st, 1814. Peleg Rogers prays to prove a bill of sale from John Kinsey to William Stone. Granted.

Edward Cowan, orphan of Elijah Cowan, deceased, chooses his brother, William Cowan, guardian, Stephen Cowan, ditto, chooses Edward Adams as guardian.

On motion of Walton Harris, attorney, Battle Mayfield is appointed guardian to Fanny McCarrel, an infant bastard child, sworn to Battle Mayfield.

James Kolb, 12 years old, orphan son of Jonothan Kolb, deceased, bound to Abraham Scott. Susannah Kolb, ditto, three years old, bound to David Witt.

John Lovejoy, Exr. of estate of Thomas Ward, in right of his wife, having given nine months notice in the Georgia Journal asks to sell 239 acres in Richmond Cty., allowed to sell said land at the Market House in Augusta.

Sept. 4, 1814. Walton Harris, acting as adm. with Hugh Montgomery, on the estate of John Hanson?, decd. claims they cannot make returns because of a demand against the estate by Edward Paine, Esquire.

Thomas Holland, appointed guardian to one infant bastard male child by name of Strother made his oath(by) of the mother Polly Whitlock.

William Cowan, now 21 years old, asks that the estate left by his father, Elijah Cowan, decd. be turned over to him and that he be accepted guardian to his brother, Edwin Cowan. Granted.

Edward Adams, guardian for Stephen Cowan and Prudence Cowan, notified that said William Cowan will ask that said estate be divided. Charles Kinney, Hardy Strickland, Ambrose Yarborough, Owen J. Bowen and Andrew Thompson, appointed Commissioners to divide said estate.

Nov. 7th, 1814. Henry and Polly Justus, appointed adms. on the estate of William Justus, Dec. James Cash, Security.

March term 1813. Will of Shadrack Dean, decd. proven by Owen J. Bowen and William Mackee. Shadrack Dean qualified as Exr.

Will of James Smith proven by William Ellington and William Hancock. John and James Smith qualified as Exrs.

Levina Brant, an orphan of six years, Feb. 14, last, bound to David Owens.

James Cash appointed adm. of the estate of Susannah Kolb, late of this county, deceased.

Polly Bearden, orphan, 14 months old, bound to John S. Rushton.

May 13th, 1813. Samuel Street appointed adm. of the estate of Samuel Street, decd.

RETURNS. Frederick Thompson and William Llewellyn on the estate of Robert Hughes, decd. Ezekiel Ralston on Isaac Wright. Abraham Chandler on Bailey Chandler. Hugh Montgomery on William Cureton. Jesse Bennett and Thomas Perry on Samuel Haggard.

Sally Turner, 11 years old, bound to John McConnell.

John Edwards, orphan of Charles Edwards bound to Richard Heath.

On application of Martha Wright, daughter of John Wright, decd. her mother, Alcy Wright, appointed guardian. The Ct. appoints said Alcy, guardian of Cassandra and James Carr Wright, two other orphans of John Wright, deceased.

William Wadsworth and Sally Wadsworth, orphans of Thomas Wadsworth, decd., chose their brother, John Wadsworth, as guardian. The court appointed John and Thomas Wadsworth, guardians of James and Seaborn Wadsworth, orphans of Thomas Wadsworth, decd., under 14 years of age.

Thomas Shockley, through age and infirmity, about to squander his property. Gideon Shockley appointed his guardian.

Jan. 3, 1814. On the petition of Robert Cummings, a legatee of David McCullars, in right of his wife, Ridley Cummings, formerly Ridley McCullars, daughter of said David McCullars, decd., for a division of the estate according to the will Dr. Willis Pope and George Menafee and Joseph Shields, appointed Commissioners to divide said estate and report to next Court.

Edward Cowan, son of Elijah Cowan, dec. chooses his uncle, John Stovall, guardian The court having appointed Benjamin Stovall as guardian for Stephen Cowan, another orphan of said decd., under 14 years old.

Mar. 4th, 1811. James R. McCleskey and Green Wood obtained letters of adm. on estate of Ethelred Wood, deceased.

March 4th, 1811. [disregard]

Levi Lowry, guardian of orphans of David McCullars, makes returns for 1810.

Thomas Hyde, appointed adm. on the estate of Robert Hodge, deceased.
[should be Robert Hyde]

Letters of adm. to Nancy C o o k on the estate of Allen Cook, deceased.

James Rogers, guardian of John Rogers, orphan of John Rogers, decd. made returns

Shadrack Humphries, one of the adms. of Joseph Humphries, made returns.

July 1st, 1811. Nathaniel Jarrett appt. adm. of Howell Jarrett, late of this Cty. deceased.

Margaret McMullen obtained letters of adm. on the estate of Samuel McMullen, deceased.

L a s t will of Samuel Haggard, late of this county, deceased, proven by the oath of Solomon Stephens. Ditto of Henry Snow, proven by John C. Watkins, Joel and Jane Jetton.

Frederick Thompson, one of the Exrs. of John Morris, made returns of inventory of the estate.

James Shields, adm. of Patrick Shields estate, made returns.

RETURNS made by: Hugh Montgomery, adm. of William Cureton. John Carmichael, adm. of Thomas Morgan. Hardy Strickland, adm. of Henry Strickland. Willis Thurmond adm. of Thomas Thurmond.

Sally a n d Nancy Morris, orphans, asks that Major James M. C. Montgomery be appt. their guardian. Granted.

George, Polly and Nancy Shields, orphans of Patrick Shields, asks that Joseph Shields, their grandfather a n d James Shields, their uncle, be appointed guardians. The Court appoints Joseph and James Shields guardian for John, Betsy and Patsy Shields.

Aug. 4, 1811. George Humphries and John Bradley, dismissed as adms. of Josiah McDonald, deceased, having finished.

Presley Knight has titles to land made good, given by Josiah McDonald in his lifetime.

David Files, adm. of James Vann, decd. makes returns.

Sept. 2nd, 1811. William Beard, one of the Exrs. of Jane Beard, makes returns.

Benjamin Camp ordered to make a statement of the property of the estate of John Berry, deceased, in his hands, and he is appointed guardian for said orphans Joshua, Robert, Polly, Betsy and William Berry.

Sept. 2nd, 1811. Walton Harris and Hugh Montgomery, guardians for Polly and John Henderson Rogers, orphans of Thomas Rogers deceased, asks to be relieved. Thomas Hyde and J. M. C. Montgomery appointed in their stead.

Nov. 4, 1811. Margaret McMullen, admtx. of the estate of Samuel McMullen, a n d Thomas P e r r y, Exr. of Samuel Haggard, makes returns.

March 2nd, 1812. Walton Harris and Hugh Montgomery appointed adms. of the estate of John Hanson, deceased. Ditto to Thomas Hanson on the estate of Thomas Hanson Jr. deceased. Ditto to Christiana Thomas on the estate of William Thomas, deceased.

Joseph Davis, Exr. returns on the estate of John Wright.

L a s t will of Thomas Hanson, late of this county, deceased, proven by Walton Harris and David Rogers.

Mrs. Mariah Hanson, relict a n d widow of J o h n Hanson, late of this county, deceased, appointed guardian of Julia, Virginia Hanson and John Augustus Hanson, orphans of said deceased.

L a s t will of Jacob Whitworth proven. Samuel Whitworth qualified as Exr.

John Carmichael, adm. of Thomas Morgan, deceased, makes returns.

Thomas Hanson, Sr. adm. of estate of Thomas Hanson, Jr. deceased, prays that a division of the co-partnership of the estate of Thomas Hanson, deceased, and John Hanson, deceased, be made, as does Walton Harris and Hugh Montgomery, adms. of the late John Hanson, decd. Ordered that Geo. Cowan, Joseph Shields, Joseph Little, Joseph Ratchford & James M.C. Montgomery divide said estates.

Walton Harris, counsel for adms. of estate of Henry Strickland, prays that a guardian be appointed for the orphans of said deceased, to-wit: Clement, Isaac and Nancy Strickland. Wilson Strickland appt. guardian of Clement and Isaac and Hardy Strickland appt. guardian to Nancy.

Last will of Jonothan Kolb, of this County, deceased, proven by Ephraim Lindsey amd Patrick Cook.

Alsey Wright appt. guardian for Cornelius McCarty Wright, by own choice, orphan of John Wright.

David Rogers, orphan of Thomas Rogers, late of this county, deceased, chose Thos. Hyde and James M.C. Montgomery his guardian.

Eli Whaley appointed guardian for Joshua - Robert, Polly, Betsy and William Berry, orphans of John Berry, late of this cty.

RETURNS: David H. McCleskey and Nathaniel Jarrett on the estate of Howell Jarrett. James R. McCleskey and Green Wood on the estate of Ethelred Wood.

May 4th, 1812. Nathan Fowler appt. adm. of the estate of Benjamin Jones, decd.

May 4, 1812. Amy, Joseph and Susannah Pinson, orphan children of James Pinson, shows Lewis J. DuPree, guardian. Also appointed guardian for James Pinson, orphan of said James Pinson, which is under 14 years of age.

David Dickson appointed guardian for Dickson Bailey, a minor under 14.

Ordered that the personal estate of Patrick Shields be divided into eight equal shares by the following persons: John McElhannon, James Tait, Levi Lowry John Skinner and Robert Henderson, reserving the hands of the guardian one share for Thomas Thurmond, if he should come before a proper tribunal, that the debt due D. S. McCravy by Thomas Thurmond be paid out of the estate.

July 6, 1812. Will of Elijah Cowan proven by Edward Adams, who was appointed adm. Ditto, George Bradford, William and David Bradford, qualify as Exrs.

July 7th, 1812. Stephen Tarborough, an orphan, committed to the care of John Lain until the next Court.

George Haynie applied for letters of adm. on the estate of Margaret, his late wife, formerly Margaret Holliday, refused because it appears he had relinquished all right to same.

Nov. 2, 1812. On motion of Walton Harris, attorney for adms. of estate of Henry Strickland, late of this county, decd. who are the guardians of Clement, Isaac and Nancy Strickland, heirs of said decd. proper person to be appointed to divide the personal estate. It appearing that Elizabeth Strickland had been duly notified, Granted. James Hendrix, Owen J. Bowen, Stephen Reed, Hugh Dickson, Wm. Dickson, Sampson Culpepper and Charles McKinney, or any five of them, meet at Deal's Mill Friday the 13th, inst. and proceeed to divide said estate.

RETURNS: Nathan Fowler on Benjamin Jones. George Humphries on Josiah McDonald. William Waits on Voluntine Hollingsworth. Uriah Humphries on Josiah McDonald

Tabitha Martin appointed guardian to infant female bastard child named Matilda Russell Martin. Barnabas Barron, Security.

George Shadrack and Uriah Humphries, adms. of the estate of Joseph Humphries, and George Humphries of John Bradley, adm. of Josiah McDonald apply for letters of /dismission.

Bartlett Johns, exr. estate of Ann Angel, failed to qualify.

Joseph Ratchford, who was appointed guardian for Sally White, who was in a state of insanity, ordered to deliver all the estate and take her receipt.

Jan. 4, 1813. Edward Adams elected Clerk

Mar. 1, 1813. Frederick Thomas and Wm. Llewellyn appointed adm. of Robert Hughes late of this county, deceased.

DEED RECORDS

Sept. 3rd, 1797. Samuel Gardner to Patrick Shields of Oglethrope County, 287 1/2 acres on Big Pond fork of Oconee River. Test. John Smith, John Cunningham.

Sept. 23, 1799. Samuel Gardner to Jos. Shields of Oglethorpe County, half of a bounty grant, surveyed Aug. 1st, 1794 in the name of Isham Matthews, on big pond fork Oconee River. Test. John Smith, John Cunningham.

Sept. 3rd, 1799. John Cunningham of Elbert County, to David Criswell of Oglethorpe County, 478 acres, part of a 870 a. surveyed for me Nov. 10, 1785 in Franklin Cty. Test. John Coreywell & Reuben Bennett.

Nov. 5th, 1798. Samuel Nelson and John Depriest of Elbert County to Jacob Pettijohn, of Jackson County, land on Currie's Creek, part of a grant to Howell Jarrett. Test. Wm. F. Luckie. Thomas Russell.

June 8, 1799. Charles Dougherty, Sheriff to Daniel W. Easley, lands, etc. of Micajah Williamson, deceased, in the hands of Sally Williamson, extrx., in favor of the Academy and Town of Washington, for damages made by promises broken by Micajah Williamson Jr. and Micajah Sr. in his lifetime. Test. M. Williamson, James Pittman.

May 5, 1799. Joseph Scott to Isaac Cowan, 122 acres on Currie's Creek. Test. George Hays. Joseph McCutchen.

June 11th, 1799. Micajah Benge and Wm. Hopkins, to Roger Keigle, all of Jackson County. Test. John Cobb, Arthur Foster.

Dec. 23, 1799. George Naylor of Columbia County, to John Strong of Jackson County. Test. Matthew Stone, Polydore Naylor and William Duke.

Sept. 23, 1786. Richard Call of Jefferson County, to John Carpenter, land in Franklin County. s/ Sept. 23, 1796. Test. James Wood and John Gorham.

Dec. 7, 1799. John Appling of Columbia County, to James Pittman, Esquire, of Jackson County, land on Sandy Creek, surveyed for John Appling 1785. Test. Wm. Beckham and Ignatius Few.

Dec. 10th, 1797. David Herring, Jr. of Oglethorpe County, to William Carter, of Jackson County, 144 acres on Sandy Creek. Test. Joseph Hughes, Kinchen Carter and Martin Moore.

Oct. 29, 1799. William Carter, deed of gift to Unity, Redmond, Elizabeth and Wm. Carter, children, land on Sandy Creek, for the use of wife and children, they to remain with her. [her name not given.] Test. William Chapman. John Moore.

July 12th, 1791. John Stringer of Abbeville S. C. to Elijah Brown of Pendleton S.C. 287 1/2 acres on Camp Creek, granted to said Stringer December 10, 1788. Test. John Molden, Sr., Peter Shriner, Samuel Brown.

Sept. 4, 1798. Edward Good to John Watterson, both of Elbert County, land on middle fork, Oconee River. Test. Stephen Grove and Samuel Grove.

Dec. 6, 1798. Thomas B. Jack, attorney for John Jack, both of Hancock County, to Talbot Arthur of Jackson County, 287 1/2 acres on Middle fork of Oconee River, vacant on all sides when surveyed, as will more fully appear by reference to grant to John Jack July 3rd, 1786. Test. William Hutcherson, Jesse Sparks, Absolom Rainey.

June 10th, 1799. John Cobb to William Watkins, land on Robertson's Creek. Test. Micajah Benge. Preston Runnells.

May 17, 1799. William Triplett, T.C. of Wilkes County, to Lawrence Briers, 80 a. in Franklin County, surveyed in the name of John Linch in 1784. Test. Thomas Terrell and Peter B. Terrell.

May 26th, 1798. Joseph McCutchen to Wm. McCutchen, 236 acres on Currie's Creek, for $80.00. Test. Thomas Kirkpatrick.

Oct. 17th, 1797. James R. Whitney, T.C. for Franklin County, land originally granted to Van McGilton in 1784. Test. John Bostwick, Moses Payne.

July 13, 1798. Matthew Stone and wife, Jenny, of Oglethorpe County, to John T. Duke of Jackson County, 400 acres on Oconee River. Test. James Duke. Thos. Duke.

Dec. 17th, 1798. Josiah N. Kennedy and wife Sarah, of Warren County, to George Whitsell of Oglethorpe County, 287 1/2 a. part of original grant to John Henson. Test. Wm. M. Stokes.

Mar. 6th, 1798. Uriah Hardman to Jesse Willingham, both of Oglethorpe County, land on Cabin Creek, Jackson County. Test Ryland Chandler. Samuel Hardman.

Dec. 17, 1798. Samuel Gardner of Jackson County, to John Cobb of Jefferson County, land in Oglethorpe County, on Cloud's Creek, surveyed for Samuel Gardner in 1785. Test. E. Hargrove and John Reynolds.

June 9, 1799. Charles Dougherty, Sheriff, to George Sibbald of Augusta, Richmond County, following lands attached June 21st, 1798. 7,000 acres granted to Micajah Williamson, Sr., May 24th, 1792. 6,000 acres granted to Abraham Thompson, same date. 920 acres each to Ralph Smith, Joseph Smellers & Janmes Ellison. 2,000 acres to John Smith, 7,000 acres to John Williams. 6,000 acres to John Brooks. 5,000 acres to Joseph Brown. 4,000 acres to William Anderson, etc., all property of Robert Morris and John Nichols, who were sued by John Sibbald.

Dec. 27, 1798. James R. Whitney, T.C. of Franklin County, to Benjamin Echols, of Franklin County, 287 1/2 acres surveyed in the name of Bethel Lamb 1784. Test. George Hemming, Henry Chapelier, Thomas Crews, Robert Walton.

Sept. 11th, 1800. George Weatherby of Jefferson County, to Martin Gardner of Jackson County, 100 acres on middle fork of Oconee River, originally granted to Isaac Stubbs. Test. Wm. M. Hawthorne and Andrew Hawthorne.

REMNANTS OF COURT OF ORDINARY RECORDS

//L/*/I/LL//J6hh/////////////////////////

1 8 0 9. John Gregg, orphan of George Gregg, bound to Peyton Chapman.

Samuel Wilson, to whom Mark Poulson was bound, treated him very cruelly, ordered that he be placed in the hands of Wm. Hewett.

George W. Moore prays that William M. Williamson, adm. of estate of Micajah Williamson, deceased, be required to make returns. Granted.

On motion of counsel for the adsm. of Patrick Shields, deceased, stating that the proceeds were not sufficient to support the seven orphans, being not more than $135.00. It is ordered that Jane Shields, admtx. be allowed the proceeds to date.

George Humphries and John Bradford, adms. of the estate of Josiah McDonald, be allowed to sell land in Jackson and Clarke counties.

July 2, 1810. Last will of William Cureton, late of this county, proven by the oaths of John and Hannah Wallace and Wm. McKey. Hugh Montgomery qualified as Exr.

Thomas Hyde and Cornelius McCarty obtained letters of adms. on estate of Thomas Bennett, late of this county, decd.

Returns made by Ezekiel Ralston, adm. of Isaac Wright, decd. And John Pennington, adm. Henry Ramsey, decd.

Sept. 3rd, 1810. Wilson McKinney appt. adm. of Grief Blankenship, late of this county, deceased.

John Carmichael, one of the adms. of Thomas Morgan, decd. makes returns.

George Rogers, orphan of John Rogers, decd. chose Robert Wilson as guardian.

Jan. 7, 1811. Wilson and Hardy Strickland obtains letters of adm. on estate of Henry Strickland, decd. Ditto, Harrison and Willis Thurmond on the estate of Thomas Thurmond, deceased.

The last will of Joseph Humphries proven by oaths of Job Rogers amd George Hampton.

Inventory of the estate of James Thurmond produced.

George, Shadrack and Uriah Humphries, exrs. of the will of Joseph Humphries, decd., ask for leave to rent and sell land.

John Shipp and John Pennington asks to be relieved as Securities of Nancy Cook, admtx. of Allen Cook.

Mar. 4, 1811. Last will of John Morris, proven by Joseph Camp and William Nichols

Sept. 4th, 1809. George Headen obtains letters of adm. on estate of Wm. L. Brazeal.

Ditto Nancy Cook on est. Allen Cook.

David Files, David McNair and James Brown obtain letters adm. on estate of James Vann, deceased.

James Appleby obtains letters of adm. on the estate of William Appleby, decd.

Samuel Hay, one of the adm. of William Morgan, decd., produced inventory.

William Waites, adm. of Voluntine Hollingsworth, made returns.

Martin and Malacki Cleck petitioned that John and Mary Borders, exrs. of Michael Borders give clear titles to land in Green County Tennessee.

Jan. 1, 1810. George W. Moore, adm. of Thomas Cowan, prays to sell perishable of the estate. Granted.

Ordered. Capt. Robert Martin take by his consent, John Holliday, orphan boy of Jeremiah Holliday, under his protection, etc. without charge to said estate. Wiley Ross and Absolom Venable ordered to sell slaves of the estate of Jeremiah Holliday

Thomas Hyde, Esquire, appointed overseer of the poor in place of D.S. McCrary who resigned.

Returns of estate of Patrick Shields by Jane and James Shields.

Feb. 10, 1810. Hugh Montgomery and Edward Adams, appointed guardians for orphans of Jeremiah Holliday, to-wit: Fanny, Nancy and Martin Holliday by their choice Court appointed them to guardian John Morton Holliday.

Upon a full consideration of the writinf of James Vann purporting to be a will and also a decree of the Chiefs and Warriors in the counsel, revoking, annuling and setting aside the said writing, determining the same is not agreeable to the rules and regulations and law of the said Nation, and it being their wish that the property should be divided among all the children of said James Vann and his widow. It is ordered that the property be disposed of as is directed by the said Councel as far as is possible. The will being considered by their Court as illegal and of no effect, and that David Files Esquire, be sworn in as adm. of the estate with the exception of said writing and that the desire of the said Nation be entered upon the Minutes of the Court.

Mar. 3, 1806. Present: B. Harris, James Hendrix, George Conway, George Humphries. John Bradley and James McDonald apply for and receive letters of adm. on estate of Josiah McDonald, deceased.

John, James and Alexander McHargus? apply for a n d receive letters of adm. on the estate of Nehemiah Smith, decd.

William Armour and Joseph Cowden obtain letters of adm. on estate of James Armour deceased.

On motion of Mrs. Ann Holmes, the mother of Arthur and Josiah Patterson, orphans of William Patterson, stating that the said orphans h a v e no person to look after their education, etc. William Barnett is appointed guardian.

Last will a n d testament of Johnson Clark produced, proven and recorded.

May 5, 1806. Sarah Wadsworth and Benjamin Watts obtains letters of adm. on the estate of Thomas Wadsworth, deceased.

Bozeman A d a i r appointed guardian to Susannah Adair, orphan of John Adair, decd.

July 9, 1806. James Eaton, son of Sally Eaton, bound to Patrick Cash for 18 yrs.

Carter Hammett bound to Mason Ezzard for 15 years.

David McCurdy, Esquire, one of the Exrs. of Johnson Clark, decd., made returns.

James Thurmond and Nancy Thurmond, his wife, formerly the wife of John Rogers, decd., the mother of three children: Milly, George a n d Zilla, heirs and orphans of John Rogers, decd., obtain letters of guardianship on said orphans.

Sept. 2, 1806. It being represented to this Court that Miles, Charlotte, Nelson and Jackson Anderson, minors and orphans of Nathan Anderson, decd., are destitute of some proper person to take charge of their estate. Sylvester Nelson is appointed guardian.

Elizabeth Kirklin obtains letters of adm. on the estate of William Kirklin, deceased.

John Clark obtains letters of adm. on the estate of John Clark, deceased.

Samuel Patton prays that Jane Carson be appointed adm. of Joseph Carson, decd.

Richard Anderson failing to make due returns on the estate of Nathan Anderson, is ordered to appear at next Court.

[about 1814]. Last will of Peter Boyles deceased, proven.

Last will of Charles Weatherford, decd. proven.

It appearing t h a t the real estate of James Hendrix, decd. is barely sufficient for the support of the widow and orphans, she is allowed to have the land for the ensuing year.

Returns: James Cash on estate of Jonothan Kolb. Samuel Street on the estate of Samuel Street.

Division of the estate of Jeremiah Holliday granted on motion of Walton Harris, attorney for Martin Holliday, one of the heirs.

June 2, 1815. Edward Adams elected Clk.

RETURNS: Abraham Chandler, adm. of Bailey Chandler. George Humphries, adm. estate of Joseph Humphries. William Cates adm. of estate of John Berry.

William Bradford adm. of Geo. Bradford.

Feb. 6th, 1815. David Rogers appointed joint guardian with James M. C. Montgomery for Polly and John Henderson Rogers, orphans of Thomas Rogers, deceased.

Verbal w i l l of James Elmore, late of this county, decd., proven. Simeon White appointed adm.

George D. Lester and Priscilla Lester, appt. guardians to Priscilla, Esther and Mahala Morgan, orphan children of William Morgan, decd., under 14 years. William Morgan, over 14, orphan son of William Morgan, decd. chooses Joseph McLester as guardian. Samuel Hay appointed guardian of Jesse Morgan, orphan of Wm. Morgan.

Mar. 6th, 1815. Hugh Montgomery and Edward Adams, guardian of orphans of Jeremiah Holliday, deceased, allowed to sell 202 1/2 acres in Twiggs County Ga.

William Harris, attorney, permitted to sell slaves belonging to the estate of James Elmore, deceased.

Will of Alexander Harper proven. Tabitha Harper qualified as Extrx.
[Harper's will not found]

Mar. 1, 1815. Returns: Lin Lowry, gdn. of orphans of David McCull/ar. William Strickland, adm. Henry Strickland.

Thomas Watson, guardian of orphans of Thomas Ward.

Joseph J. Scott, adm. of Thomas Carson, prays to be dismissed.

Rebecca Kolb, orphan of Jonothan Kolb, chose David.W/itt, guardian and he is appointed guardian of Polly Kolb, her sister. James Kolb, 13 years old orphan of Jonothan Kolb, bound to Jonothan McLester to learn hatter's trade.

July 3rd, 1815. William Payton applies for letters of adm. on estate of Letha Catchings, late of Jackson County, decd. She being the wife of Meredith C. Catchings, and he in life, refused.

Aug. 15, 1815. Benjamin Briant appt. adm. of William Gilmore, deceased.

Robert and William Allen, legatees of William Allen, deceased, asks for division and Joseph Little, James Appleby, Edward Adams, Thomas Niblack and Absolom Wofford appointed commissioners.

Nancy Blackwell, adm. of estate of Ambrose Blackwell, makes returns.

Sept. 4th, 1815. Rachael Deal appointed adm. of Wm.. Deal, late of daid county, deceased.

Hugh Montgomery, Exr. of William Allen, deceased, made returns.

Hugh Montgomery and Walton Harris, adm. of estate of John Hanson, decd. asked to be dismissed. Granted.

Will of Manning Gore proven by David and William Hudson.[will not found].

Oct. 2, 1815. Nathan Johnson appointed adm. of William Sharp, late of this cty.

Susannah Benton, daughter of Modecai Benton, deceased, chooses James Pittman as guardian. [Mordecai]

Feb. 6th, 1816. Returns: Henry Johnson, adm. of William Sharp. Hannah Hendrix and Fanny Wilson, admx. of James Hendrix. Rachael Deal, admx. of Wm. Deal. Colonel R. Jones, adm. estate of G.W.Parks.

David H. McCleskey and Daniel Jarrett, adm. of Howell Jarrett, permission to sell real estate.

Avilla?Sharp, widow of Wm. Sharp, takes her dower. John Pittman, Wm. Matthews, Wm. Jones, Zachariah Lay, James J. Moore, James and John Smith, commissioners to lay it off.

Simeon White leave to sell real estate of James Elmore, deceased.

Battle Mayfield appointed adm. of estate of Moses Snow.

VARDY MOTE bound to Jesse Grizzle for four years to learn blacksmith's trade.

Henry Sutton bound to David S.M.McCravy.

Mar. 4, 1816. Polly Langley and Elisha Lolly/ or Lotty appointed adm. of estate of Oswell Langley, deceased.

Battle Mayfield ordered to make returns as guardian of Fanny Carrel, a bastard child.

Nancy Hodge, formerly Nancy Scott makes returns on estate of Andrew Scott.

RETURNS: Nathaniel Jarrett, adm. of Howell Jarrett. Alexander Cowan, adm. of Wm. Cook. James Cash, Exr. of Jonothan Kolb amd adm. of Susannah Kolb.

Ordered to come before the Court prepared to settle these estates: Ordered that Nathan Camp a n d Elizabeth Howard, formerly Elizabeth Gideon and Hardy Howard who seemed to have had a hand in the management of estate of James Gideon, deceased, come forward and render an account of said estate.

May 6, 1816. James Akin applied as adm. of Samuel Akin, deceased.

Susannah Pierce applied as admx. of Wm. Pearce, deceased. [Pearce]

Beverly Pirkerson applied as adm. of John H. Skinner, deceased.

Will of James Orr and Joseph Culperrer, proven.

James Cash m a d e returns on estate of Jonothan Kolb.

Margaret McMillen, admx. estate of Saml McMillen, allowed to sell two slaves.

Hosea Gideon, orphan of James Gideon, deceased, chooses Hosea Camp guardian and Hosea Camp is appointed guardian for Berry Gideon, another orphan of said decd.

Polly Slaton, orphan daughter of Mary Slaton, decd. chooses her brother, Fleming Slaton as guardian.

July 1st, 1816. David Rogers appointed adm. de bonis non on estate of Jacob Gray deceased.

Patsy Jarrett appointed admx. on the estate of Nicholas Jarrett, decd.

Samuel Knox appointed adm. on estate of John Knox, deceased.

James H. Kidd appointed adm. of estate of James Kidd, deceased.

Sept. 2, 1816. William Wiley appointed adm. on estate of George Poyner, decd.

Zeno and Malissa Perkins, minor orphans of Constantine Perkins, late of Morgan County, deceased, are now living in the county and have no proper person to take care of them. Ordered that Sally Perkins and David Boring be appointed guardians.

Will of John Adams proven. Will of Wm. Hickman proven.

Nancy Blackwell, adm. of Ambrose Blackwell, makes returns.

John T. Creswell appointed adm. of David Creswell, deceased.

Cornelius McCarty and Thomas Hyde, adm. of Thomas Bennett applies for letters of dismission.

David Witt and William Potts appointed guardians of Harmon, James, Jonothan and Richard Kolb, orphan children of Jonothan Kolb, deceased.

Nov. 4th, 1816. Hardy Howard appointed adm. of Samuel Street, deceased.

January 6, 1817. Edwards Adams, elected Clerk.

Ezekiel Gancy? appointed adm. of Chas. Gancy? deceased, of said county.

David Castleberry and Joshua Hill, appt. adm. of estate of Edward Hill, late of said county, deceased.

RETURNS made: Nathan Johnson adm. of William Sharp. George Humphries, adm. of Joseph Humphries. James Cowan, adm. of John Adams. Samuel Street, adm. of Samuel Street. Beverly Pirkerson, adm. of John S. Skinner.

Jan. 7, 1817. Elizabeth Jack, appointed adm. of Wm. Jack, late of this county, deceased.

Hardy Howard, adm. of Samuel Stewart, deceased, asks that a slave woman belonging to the estate, having committed an offense which would forfeit her life, be sold at a private sale.

WILL. Ruth Stapler. s/ Apr. 11, 1835. p/ Sept. 7, 1835. Sons: Amos, John, Robert, Thomas and William Stapler. Daughters: Sarah Owens, Mary Hutchinson; the children of Elizabeth Norman, deceased : Frances Rogers, Rachael Strickland a n d Nancy Rogers. Son John Stapler and grand son Thomas L. Stapler, Exrs. Test. Wm. Simpkins, Benjamin Simpkins, William G. Stapler.

WILL. Thomas Neil. s/ Apr. 9, 1813. p/ Nov. 3rd, 1823. Wife Ruth. Daughter Peggy Wilkes Neil, under age. Test. James McBee and Thomas Baird?, John McDown. Wife Ruth and Joseph Barr, Exrs.

WILL. Richard Winters. s/ May 28, 1826. p/ July 3rd, 1826. My son, John Hampton Winters. My two daughters: Susan Emeline and Elizabeth Ann Winters a n d my last wife Betsy, formerly Betsy Hays, and her child, Martha Adeline. Test John Winters Sr., G.W. Winters and Geo. N. Hampton.

MISCELLANEOUS RECORDS JACKSON COUNTY GEORGIA

INDEX

W. INDICATES WILL. A given name may appear several times on one page.

ABERNATHY, John 26, 27. Clary 26.
ADAIR [also Adare], Bozeman 10,11,18,63.
" Jacob 39. James 41. John 63. Jos. 25.
" Mary 41. Robert 11. Susannah 63.
" Ruth 39. Wm. 41.
ADAMS, Asenith 19. Caroline 20. Edward 4,
" 6, 10,17,18,25,24,35,36,37,38,56,57,59,
" 60, 62,63,64. Eliza 60. Geo. 24. G.F.20,
" John 37(w),65. Penelope 19. Thos. 19.
" Thomas RG. 20(w).
AKIN, James 65 , Peter 16. Samuel 65.
ALBERT, G.W. 18.
ALEXANDER, Adly 35. James 53.
ALFORD, James 4
ALLEN, Amelia 19, Asa 19, Benj. 40,
" Daniel 28, Dianna 20, Eliza 35, Gray 19
" Robert 20, 64. Washington 6. Wm. 3,35(w)
" 64.
ALLISON, Elinor 5, 6. Jas. 5(w), Jas.S.
" 5. John 33, 53. Lucia 5. Paschal 5.
" Samuel 5.
ANDERSON, Charlotte 63. Gabriel 34.
" Jackson 63. Miles 63. Nathan 11,63.
" Nelson 63. Patsy 36. Richard 11,63.
" William 8, 69.
ANGEL, Ann 36(w), 60.
ANGLIN, Henry 21,26,28. Peter 26. Polly 25
ANTHONY, Ezekiel 51,52. Martin 7, 51.
" Mary 51(w). Thomas 51. Wade 51.
" Willis 51.
APPERSON, Anderson 24. Robert 24
APPLEBY, H.C. 48. James 14,62,64.
" John 7, 12,25. Louisa 48, Virginia 12.
" William 6,20,51,52,62.
APPLING, Eleanor 45. John 39,45,60.
ARCHER, Eliza 20. Harry 13.
ARMOUR, James 37,63. Wm. 37,63.
ARMSTRONG, Jas. 23,26,29,31,39. John 21,
" Rhoda 37.
ARNOLD, Cammy 7. Stephen 7.
ARTHUR, Talbot 16,27,30,31,45,54,60.
ASHWORTH, Benj. 39.
ATKINSON, Agrippa 43.
AUBRY, Phillip 44.
AVARY/AVERY, Betsy 5. Phillip 5(w)
" Rebecca 5. Thos. 5. Wm. 5.

BACON, Eliza 13. Sarah 19.
BAGBY, Betsy 35, Geo. 4, 35(w). Henry 35
" John 35. Jos. 35. Miriam 35. Thos.35.
" William 35.
BAGGETT, John 11.
BAILEY/BAILY, A. 14. Betsy 5. Caroline
" 40. Dickson 5,59. James 40. John 40.
" Mary 56. Richard 1. Robert 5,30,40.
" Thomas 56.
BANKS, Thomas 56.
BANKSTON, A. 1, Abner 29. Jas. 23.
" Thomas 55. Wm. 30.
BARBER, Matthew 15.
BARKER, Eldridge 6, Gray 6. Isham 6.
" Lewis 6(w). Robert 32. Rusell 14.
" Urvil 6.
BARNES, Thos. 13,20.
BARNETT, Claborn 55. James 27, John 1,12,
" 21,22,26,28,32,33,38,39,54,55.
" Margt. 6. Mial J. 22, 26,38. Nathan 55.
" Polly 26. Samuel Sr. 6(w). Samuel 6,11,
" 55. Wm. 2,33,63. Zachariah 26.
BARR, James 14(w),25,36,43. Jas.H.48.
" Mary 14.
BARRON, Amanda 13. Barnabas 25,59.
" Calvin 13, 48. Eliza 13. Isaac 13.
" John 23,32. Marshall 13. Nancy 13,23,
" 48. Sally 13. Samuel 13. Thos.13,26,
" 48(w). Wm. 13, 48.
BAUGH, Bartley 6. Daniel 6. Henry 6.
" Jeremiah 6. Josiah 6(w). Sarah 6.
BAXTER, Andrew 17,34.
BAYLISS, Betsy 3. Isham 3.
BEALL, Daniel 21.
BEARD, Alexa 36. Eliza 36. Geo.36.
" Janett 36(w). Jean 36,43. Jane 58.
" Mary 36/ Thos. 36. Wm. 36, 58.
BEARDEN, Polly 57.
BEART, Henry 43.
BEATY, Mttie 5.
BEATTY, Chas. 36. Thomas 22.
BEAUCHAMP, Abisha 38. John 54.
BEAVERS, Eliza 59. Jas. 25(w) Jane 35.
" John 35,36. Jos. 35. Martha 25. Mary 25
" Patsy 35, Reuben 35,36. Robert 11, 35(w)
" Sally 35. Silas 35. Susannah 35. Wm.13(w)

I

INDEX

BECKHAM, William 2, 60.
BELL, Andrew 32, 38. Eleanor 7. Jackson
" 41,51. Martha 40. Walter 28. Wm. 6,7,
" 20, 41.
BENDER, John 12.
BENGE, Micajah 1,12,23,33,54,56,60,61.
BENNETT, Asa 18. Bartley 18. Eliza 13.
" Hezekiah 18. H.A. 48. Jeptha 24. Jesse 5,
" 54,27. Micajah 24(w). Neriah 13,
" Patsy 13,18. Peter 24. Rachael 18.
" Reuben 60. Thomas 18,49,61,65. Wm. 18(w)
" 24.
BENNING, John 15. Joseph 15.
BENTLEY, Jeremiah 33.
BENTON, Floyd 52. John 46. Levi 14.
" Mary 46. Mordecai 33,64. Nancy 46.
" Susannah 64.
BERRY, Ann 6. Betsy 58,59. Eliza 10,35.
" John 4,10,11,35(w),58,59,63. Joshua 11,
" 35,58. Martha 35. Mary 10,35.
" Polly 58,59. Robt. 10,11,35,58,59.
" Susannah 23. Wm. 11,23,35,58,59.
BETTS, Isaac Sr. 24. John 24. Joshua 11.
" Nelly 24. Reddick 14.
BIBB, William 34.
BICKLEY, Jas. 45.
BILLUPS, John 56.
BISHOP, James 25. Stephen 54. Thos.54.
BLACK, John 28,31. Margt. 14.Thos.14(w).
" Samuel 14. Caroline 14. Cynthia 14.
" Amelia 14. Hugh 14. Augustine 14.
" Virginia 14.
BLACKBURN, Augustine 17,22,23,24,27.
" Austin 16. John 24. Nancy 27. Wm.16,23.
BLACKWELL, Agnes 36. Ambrose 36,44,64,65.
" Nancy 44,64,65. James 49.
BLACKSTOCK, Mary 24.
BLAIR, Elizabeth 50.
BLALOCK, Calvin 47. Dolly 18. Josiah 47(w)
" Mary 47. Margt. 47. Susan 47. Wm. 47.
BLANKENSHIP, Grief 61.
BLASINGAME, John 45.
BOND, Wm. 23.
BOOKER, Gideon 2. Wm. 2.
BOOTH, James 53(w). John 53. Sarah 53.
BORDERS, Ann 12. Cynthia 8. Enoch 12,47.
" Isaac 35,47(w). John 12,35,47,56.
" Lucinda 12. Malinda 12. Mary 24,35,62.
" Matilda 12. Michael 3,12,35(w),43,47,
" 56, 62. Phoebe 35. Polly 12. Ruth 35.

BORDERS, Stephen 12(w),24,35. Wm.24.
BORING, David 65. Isaac 8,19(w).
" James 36. John 5,6,19,36. Phoebe 19.
" Robert 19. Wm. 40.
BOSTAIN, Eliza 24. Hannah 24. Jacob 24.
" Matthew 24(w). Peggy 24. Sarah 24.
BOSTON, John 32.
BOSTWICK, John 34, 61.
BOSWORTH, Elizabeth 51.
BOWDEN, Lucinda 47. Wm. 47.
BOWEN, Hiram 25. Horatio 25. Joel 54.
" Nancy 25. Owen J. 25(w),34,36,38,57,
" 59, Perry 12,25,50. Thos. 25,37,50.
BOYD, John 54, Wm. 21.
BOYLE, Catherine 37. Eliza 24. John 37.
" Hannah 37. Peter 37(w),63. Rebecca 37.
" Robert 37.
BRADFORD, David 18,36,59. Geo. 18,36(w),
" 59,63. James 36. John 61. Mary 36.
" Nancy 36. Wm. 36,43,59,63.
BRADLEY, Abraham 15. John 58,59,63.
" Joseph 24. Josiah 24. Susannah 49.
" Thomas 49.
BRADSHAW, John 53.
BRANHAM, Spencer 39.
BRANT, Levina 57.
BRASELTON, Amos 7. Daniel 7. Gustavus 41.
" D. 41. Henry 7. Jacob 7(w),14,41,42.
" Job 7. John 7. Malissa 52. Reuben 7.
" William 7.
BRAZEAL, Alexa 6. Britton 24. Eliza 18(w),
" 25. Frederick 25(w),37. John 6, 36.
" Lucy 6. Penelope 26. Polly 36. Rebecca
" 7. Sally 36. Washington 14. Wm. 6,32,62.
BREWER, George 15.
BRIDGEWATER, Samuel 28,30.
BRIERS, Lawrence 61.
BRIGGS, Zebediah 54.
BRIGHTWELL, Theodore 39.
BROADWELL, Jesse 25.
BROCK, James 46
BROOKER, Eliza 53. James 53.
BROOKS, Alfred 42. James 26. Jarrett 47.
" John 61. Littleberry 8. Magmus 7,8,18,25.
" Middleton 47(w). M.A. 12,13. Rachael 35.
" Stephen 10. W.A. 50.
BROWN, Bedford 34. Betsy 52. Betty 16,B.F.46.
" Elijah 60. James 2,33,62. John 29.Jos. 61.
" Lemuel 52(w). Samuel 53. Sarah 5,51,60.
" Thos. 16,29,51,52,53. Tillman 52.

INDEX

BRUCE, Thomas 24.
BRUZEL, Reves 5.
BRYAN, Moses 50.
BRYANT/BRIANT, Archibald 22. Archelius 34.
" Benjamin 18,23,64. Esther 37. Mary A.13.
" Sarah 18,23.
BUCKLEY, James 16.
BURFORD, Solomon 45.
BURK, Robert 21,54.
BURKSDALE, Daniel 1.
BURNS, D.M. 8.
BURSON, Brookfield 26,53. B.F.51.
" David 26. Elisha 26. Isaac 26(w)
" Joseph 26. Sarah 26.
BURTON, Caleb 1. Robert 1
BUTLER, Daniel 16,27. General 47.
" Hester 47. James 47. Matilda 47.
" Sarah 47.
BYERS, Wm. 33, Wm. Jr. 33.

CAIN, Polly 46
CALL, Richard 1,3,60.
CALLAHAN, Edward 53, Jacob 19.
CAMERON, Ambrose 27
CAMP, Benj. 58. D.T.47. Hosea 37,43.
" Joseph 62. Nathan 10,65. Richard 16.
" Thomas 4, 35.
CAMPBELL, Benj 43. Duncan 4,44. Robert
" 9,10,23,28,29,30,33,39. Wm. 34.
CANDLER, Henry 1.
CARLTON, Gabriel 31. Henry 31. Thos.45.
CARMICHAEL, Duncan 6. John 4,6(w),58,59,
" 62. John Jr. 6.
CARNES, Thomas 56.
CARPENTER, John 60.
CARR, Patsy 37.
CAREL,CARRELL/CAROL/CARROLL, Fanny 64,
" James 37(w), John 37. J.M.18. Sara 37.
CARRINGTON, Robert 15.
CARSON, Jane 63. Jos. 39,63. Thos.4,12,
" 64.
CARTER, Eliza 34,60.Geter 3. Henry 54.
" H.C. 41. Jacob 30c,55. John 34(w),56.
" Kinchen 60. Redmond 60. Robt. 1.
" Solomon 9,10. Solomon Sr. 10,
" Solomon Jr. 10. Unity 60. Wm.10,22,29,
" 33,45,54,60. Wm.P. 53. W. 12.
CASEY, John 18,55. P.P.48.

CASH, Benj. 41, Geo. 41. James 53,57,
" 63,64. Joel 41. Martha 41. Patrick
" 53,63. John 37,41(w).
CASTLEBERRY, Claborn 36,43. David 28,
" 34,65. Jacob 2. Lucretia 37. Mark 37.
" Mary 2. Odam 37. Richard 34. Sara 37.
" Thomas 4,34. Wm. 37(w).
CATCHINGS, Luther 64. Meredith 64.
CATES, Wm. 4,11,63.
CAVIN, Malinda 19. Wm. 19.
CECIL, Leonard 14.
CHANDLER, Abraham 34,44,57,63.
" Bailey 6,44,48,57,63. Dudley 51.
" Early 13. Edith 51. Eliza 13.
" Henry 34. Jos. 12. Merritt 13.
" Nancy 46.Parks 6,29. Ryland 61.
" Solomon 12. Sterling 51(w)
" Tabitha 13(w),36.
CHAPELIER, Henry 56,61.
CHAPMAN, John 34. Payton 61. Wm.38,60.
CHEATHAM, Chas. 7, John 50.
CHEELY, Richard 13.
CHESLEY, Amanda C. 13.
CHRISTIAN, Harriett 36.
CHRISTMAS, B. 31. R. 34.
CHURCH, Gabriel B. 8. Sarah 8.
CLARDY, A.V. 24.
CLARK, Caroline 12. James 4,34. John 4,
" 20, 63. Johnson 31,35(w),63. Patsy 4,
" 35. Sarah 35. Thos. 38.
CLARKSTON, Jos. 29,30,32,55.
CLAXTON, Jos. 44.
CLECK/CLACK, Malachi 43,62. Martin
" 43,62. Mary 35.
CLEMENTS, Bishop 37.
CLEVELAND, Benj. 19.
CLIETT, Isaac 2.
CLOUD, Eliza 46.
CLOWER, Elijah 20.
COBB, John 2,12,14,15,26,39,55,60,61.
" Jacob 40. Missouri 40. Peter 54.
COCHRAN, James 9(w),42. Mary 14(w),42.
COGBURN, James 55.
COHOON, Geo. 32
COLEMAN, Eliza 38. John 38(w), 45.
COLLIER, Edward 39. Sarah 20.
COLLING, Jos. 23.

INDEX

COLLINS, Abraham 24. Eliza 24. Henry 24.
" John 24. Priscilla 24. Sarah 24,
" Stephen 1, Zachariah 24(w).
COLTON, Sally 24.
COMBS, Aaron 18. May 38. Nancy 38. Wm.38.
CONNER, Daniel 23.
CONWAY, Geo. 63.
COOK, Allen 58,62. Eliza 4, Hannh 5.
" Henry 29. John 51. Jonothan 4.
" Jos. 54. Nancy 58,62. Patrick 59.
" Shem 54. Wm. 64.
COOPER, James 22. Mildred 4.
CORCORAN, Thos 22,26.
COREYELL, John 60.
COSBY, Sydnor 27.
COVEN, Forgy 43.
COWAN, Alexa 64. Edward 36,56,57.
" Elijah 5,36(w),43,56,57,59.
" Geo. 28,59. Isaac 11,37,38,44,60.
" James 37,65. Sarah 36. Marjorie 38.
" Prudence 36,57. Stephen 36,56,57.
" Thomas 1,62. Wm. 36,57.
COWDEN, Jos. 63.
COWDER, Edward 40.
COWLING, Benj. 17,23. Jos. 17.
COX, John 22. Middleton 13. Susannah
" 16,31. Zachariah 22,32,45,54.
CRAFT, Daniel 46,53. Hannah 46(w),53.
" Martha 46. Mary 46. Polly 53(w)
" Rebecca 46,53.
CRAWFORD, Arthur 34. Chas. 20. Claborn 33.
" Ebeneze 20. Eliza 42. Henry 7. Jas.20.
" John 20. Peter 33. Polly 20. Sarah 20.
" Thomas 20.
CREIGHTON, Eliza 6,46. John 6,20,46,49.
CRISLER, Abram 18. Absolom 18,25,48(w).
" Anna 48. Jeptha 48,53. Jonothan 18.
" Joel 48.
CRISWELL/CRESWELL, David 27,60,65. D.18,
" 40. John 65. Robert 40.
CROLL, James 9.
CROW, Jacob 4. Jacob Jr. 4. Lewis 4.
CRUSE, Thomas 56,61.
CULPEPPER, Henry 37. Joseph 37(w),65.
" Malachi 15. Nancy 37. Sally 37.
" Sampson 59. Simeon 37.
CUMMINGS, Ridley 57. Robert 57. Thos.53.
CUNNINGHAM, Agnes 50. Amanda 50.
" Andrew 7,8,21(w),33,50. Ansel 13(w),
" 24,48. Columbus 50. Drury 13.

CUNNINGHAM - continued
" Elizabeth 7(w),21. Hugh 21,50.
" H.M. 50. James 7,19,47. Jane 50.
" John 13,14,21,29ϕ, 32,38,39,48⅄,50,
" 60. Joseph 5,7,8,21,50(w), J.20.
" J.H. 42,48. Margt. 21. Mary 13,48(w),
" Wm. 13,48.
CURETON, Martha 36(w). William 57,58,61.
CURRY, Thomas 31.
CUTLIFF, John 46.

DABB, Joseph 39.
DALE, Stephen 25.
DALTON, John 49(w), Sarah 49. Vinstron 49.
DAMRON, Chas. 25(w). Nancy 26. Peggy 26.
" Polly 25. Uriah 25.
DANELLY, James 3.
DANIEL, Allen 19,33,39. James 12. Mary 45.
" Polly 19. Wm. 19,30,33,45.
DARDEN, John 26.
DAVID, Francis 41. Isaac 51. Haden 41.
" Joseph 14.
DAVIDSON, Chas. 15. Julius 15. Philemon 15.
DAVIE, Joseph 35.
DAVIS, Emily 51. Isham 33. Joseph 6,24,37,
" 42,43,44,48(w),56,58. Nancy 54. Thos.14,
" 47. Wm. 38,54.
DEAKINS, Wm. Jr. 22,26.
DEAL, Elinor 11. Ephriam 3. Jarvis 35.
" Jemima 32,35,40. Lewis 11. Nancy 11.
" Rachael 64. Stephen 11. Wm. 11,28,31,32,
" 35(w), 40,44,64.
DEAN/DEEN, Arche 38. Burkell 55. Eupharance
" 38. Frederick 38. Jacob 38. John 38.
" Mourning 38. Nathaniel 38,55. Shadrack
" 38(w),57. Thomas 38.
DELAPRIERRE, Angie 14. Mary 14,41.
DENT, Geo. 14.
DEPRIEST, James 33. Jane 32. John 32,33,
" 54,60. J.D.24.
DERRICOTT, J. 39.
DIAMOND, John 29,31.
DICKEY, Samuel 53.
DICKSON[see Dixon also] David Sr. 37.
" David 5(w),35,36,43,56,59. Hugh 59.
" James 5. Michael 36. Samuel 5. Wm.5,59.
DILLON, Dr. Edmond 2.
DILLPORT, Nancy 49.
DIXON, Celina 14. David 17,18. Letty 14.
" William 14,20.

IV

INDEX

DOGGETT, Charlton 23.
DOOLEY, Benjamin 45.
DORSEY, Jacob 1. Seakin 1.
DOSS, Claborn 28. Edward 21. Geo. 5,7,21.
" Green 21. James 21. Jane 7. Jarrett 21.
" Jinny 7. John 2,7,21. Joseph 21.
" Mary 7. Sarah 7.
"DOUGHERTY/DAUGHTERTY, Chas. Sr. 13,18,
" 42,52(w),53,56. Chas. Jr. 18,42,52.
" Charles 6,13,16,21,27,31,32,39,54,
" 60,61. Eliza 13,18. James 13. Rebecca 18.
DRANE, H. 12.
DREADON, Jonothan 35.
DUKE, Green 52. Henry 46. James 61.
" John 3,61. Taylor 44. Thos. Sr. 12,27.
" Thomas 61. Wm. 12,26,32,38,47,60.
DUNN, Jenny 37. John 39.
DUNSON, Linton 49. Rosanna 48.
DUPREE, Charles 13. Lewis 59.
DURBIN, Luke 10,30,43. Sarah 10,43.
DYER, Sarah 8.
DYKES, Isaac 37.

EAKIN, Geo. 35. Jane 35. Samuel 35.
EARLY, Jeffrey 1,16.
EARNEST, Jacob 54.
EASLEY, Benj 15,27,29,45. B. 29,53.
" Daniel 27,28,30,32,34,40,60. Esther 38.
" Richard 34. Robert 29. Roderick 15,23,
" 26,32,45,53. R. 15,21,39,55.
EAST, Joseph 16,22,29,31. Milly 16,22.
EASTEN, Reuben 54.
EATON, James 63. Sally 63.
ECHOLS, Benj 37,56,61. Eliza 37.
EDMONDSON, Wm. 54.
EDWARDS, Charles 57. Edmond 30. John 57.
" Rachael 38.
ELBERT, Samuel 23.
ELDER, Edmond S. 46. Susan 46. Wm.49.
ELLINGTON, Wm. 36,57.
ELLIS, Mary 1, Radford 22,29. Solomon 1.
" William 22.
ELLISON, James 61. Robert 9. Samuel 51.
" Sarah 31.
ELMORE, Jsmes 37(w),63,64.
EMBRY, Boley 7(w). Hezekiah 7. John 7.
" Joseph 45. Sarah 7, Talbot 7.Tempy 7.
" Unity 7. William 7.
EPPERSON, Littleberry 29.

ERCHART, Gabriel 2.
ESKRIDGE, John M. 51.
ESPY, Elizabeth 13. John 23,29,37,40,43,
" 45. Petty 13. Robert 13.
EUBANKS, John 3. Levi 52
EVANS, Daniel 4.
EWING, James 15. Thos. 11,35,44.
EZZARD, John 4, 28. Lewis 4. Mason 10,63,
" Nancy 4. William 4.

FARABY, John 49.
FARROW, Penny 44. Perrin 44.
FEW, Alfred 20. Camillas 20,42. Ignatius
" 12, 20. I. 34,60. LaFayette 20,
" Leonidas 20(w), 42. Martha 20. Wm. 20.
" William Jr. 2.
FIELDER, John 28.
FILES, David 58,62.
FINCH, Burdette 22. Chas. 22,26.Joice 22.
/FINDLEY, Thomas 44,46.
FINLEY, Mary 8(w).
FLAGG, Chandler 19(w)
F̶L̶A̶N̶I̶G̶A̶N̶
FLANIGAN, John 6, 46.
FLEMING, John 3.
FLIPPANT, Jesse 15.
FLOURNOY, Eliza 46(w). Robert 53.
FLOYD, John 55.
FOOTMAN, Richard 2.
FORTE, Arthur 11.
FOSTER, Anderson 31. Arthur 10,40,60.
" G.W. 54. Ira 7. John 1,39,56. J.Harden
" 54. William 9,16,17.
FOWLER, Hillory 38. Leury 50. Nathan 38(w),
" 59. Tabitha 38. Thos. 50. Wm.37,50.
" Zepheniah 38.
FRANKLIN, Absolom 22. Lewis 25. Margt. 22.
FREEMAN, Ann 35. Eliza 5,50. Holman 27,31,43.
" James 31,34,50,55. John 12,30,50,51.
" Jonothan 50(w). Mariah 50. Mary 25.
" Polly 35. Sarah 50.
FROST, Johnson 5,44. Samuel 47. Wm. 47.
FULCHER, Austin 19.
FULLER, Benj 56. Isaac 55. John 54.
" Joshua 1. Mary 56.

INDEX

GAINES, G. 15
GALLOWAY, John 34.
GAMBLE, Jane 16. John 16. Robt. 16.
Samuel 16.(GAMBLE)
GANCY, Chas. 65. Ezekiel 65.
GANLEY, John 3.
GANTNALL, Francis 39.
GARBOROUGH, E.D. 48.
GARDNER, Alexa. Daniel 33. Martin 61.
" Richard 35. Samuel 1,5,10,14,23,27,28,
" 29,30,31,32,33,38,39,40,43,45,55,56,
" 60,61. Susannah 23,45.
GARNER, Charles 55. Green 8. James 8.
GARNETT, John 33.
GARRETT, Catherine 34. Eli 3. John 33,34,
" 56. Polly 8.
GARVIN, James 14.
GATES, Ann 5. Charles 54,55, Elisha 5.
" Valentine 55.
GATHRIGHT, John 52. Miles 28,29. Milly 52.
" William 51,54. Wm. M. 52(w). W.M.8,41,49
" Zebulon 52.
GAYNE, James 1.
GEORGE J. 16,27. Wm. 33.
GERRARD, Jacob 4. John 4.
GIBSON, Mary 55. Nancy 55.
GIDDENS, H.C. 41. Sally 50.
GIDEON, Berry 37,65. Eliza 10,14,37,65.
" Francis 14. Hosea 37, 65. James 10,22,
" 27,65. James Jr. 37(w). Richard 35.
GILBERT, Benj 1. John 19(w).
GILHAM, Robert 15.
GILLAM, Frances 18.
GILLELAND, Thomas 23.
GILLESPIE, Alexa 5,43. Sarah 5,43.
GILMAN, Margt. 50.
GILMER, John 54.
GILMORE, John 26. Wm. 63.
GLASCOCK, Thos. 2,54.
GLAWSON, Jincey 19.
GLAZE, John 26.
GLENN, Eliz 8. Eunice 8. James 8(w),30,31,
" 36. Jane 8. John 13. Joshua 8.
" Letitia 8. Sarah 6.
GLOVER, Ruth 34,
GOBER, H.B. 46. John 52.
GOOD, Thomas 11, 32. Edward 60.
GOODLET, James 22,35.
GOODMAN, Irena 41. John 41(w)

GOODON, Francis 30.
GOODRICK, Russell 21,33,40.
GOOLSBY, Isiah 54. Josiah 27.
GORDON, Alexa 40.
GORE/GOAR, Jacob 2. Manning 64. Rachel 2.
GORHAM, John 1,23,31,38,54,55,60.
GOWEN, Abel 38.
GRAHAM, Esther 35. James Sr. 43. James
" Jr. 43. Martin 50.
GRANT, Geo. 26.
GRANTHAM, Usby 37
GRAVES, James 1. Robert 3.
GRAY, Geo. 50. Hezekiah 27. Jacob 65.
GREEN, James 25. Jane 35. John 22,35(w)
" Margaret 35. Matilda 35. Sarah 35.
" Wm. 35,38.
GREGG, Geo. 61. John 43,61.
GRESHAM, Davis 39.
GRIFFIN, John 22,32,49. Michael 1.
GRIFFITH, Ezekiel 22. John 38. P.J.E. 42,
" Robert 38.
GRIZZLE, Jesse 64.
GROVES, Samuel 60. Stephen 60.
GUIGER, Valentine 34.
GUIRE, Phillip 26.(mCguire?)
GUNNELLS, Daniel 38. Nicholas 38.

HAGGARD, Alford 5. Frank 5. Geo. 5.
" James 5,18,51. James E. 46. John 5.
" Jonothan 5. Ruth 5. Samuel 5(w),57,58.
" Samuel Jr. 5. Susannah 5.
HAGLER, Benj 46
HAYNIE, (HAINEY) Geo. 22
HALL, Geo. 56. Eliza 8.
HAMBRICK, Burwell 11. James 23. Jos. 11,23.
" Thomas 11,23. William 10.
HAMILTON/HAMBLETON, Concord 2. Jas. 2,5,44.
" Thomas W. 2(w)
HAMMETT, Carter 63.
HAMMOND, Elvira 48.
HAMPTON, Alcy 20. Geo. 5. James 20. John9,
" 27, 29,30,54,55. Sarah 20.
HANCOCK, John 43,46,47. Samuel 8. Wm.36,
" 43,57.
HANDLEY, Derby 29.
HANNAH, John 40. Wm. 42.
HANSON, John 36,43,57,58,59,64. Julia 57.
" Mariah 57. Mary 8. Samuel 2. Thomas 4,
" 57,58,59. Thos. Jr. 36(w),58,59.

INDEX

HARBIN, Nathaniel 12.
HARDEN, John 40. Sophia 40. Swan 16,23.
HARDMAN, Samuel 61. Uriah 46,61.
" W.B.J. 47,52.
HARDY, Frances 5. Lewis 7. Presly 14.
" Preston 14.
HARE, Susy 37.
HARGROVE, Asbury 47. Eldridge 34,45,53.
" Eliza 47. E. 15,34,45,61. Henry 47.
" James 12,20,47(w),51,52,53. J.W. 49.
" Seaborn 47. Wm. 47.
HARPER, Alexa 37(w),63. Allen 44.
" Eliza 37. Geo. 30, James 29. John 47.
" Martha 37. Tabitha 37.
HARRINGTON, Drury 34.
HARRIS, Buckner 1,17,18,28, Harris.
" B. 11,16,23,29,34,39,40,63. Claborn
" 8,38. Early 36. Eliza 12. G.L.47.
" Jesse 18,25(w). Joseph 12(w). Lindy
" 28. N. 44. Timothy 28,30,33. Viney 25.
" Walton 12,17,18,25,43,49,56,57,58,59,
" 63, 64. Wm. 17,64.
HARRISON, Ann 42. Caroline 42. Coleman
" 19,51(w),53. Frances 51. Hezekiah 19.
" Jane 42. Jason 18,51. John 5,42(w).
" Joseph 19(w),48,51. Josephus 18.
" J.C.49. E. 51. Margt. 42. Mary 42.
" Sarah 42. Thaddeus 51. Thomas 42.
" Tillman 18. T.M.53. Wm. 42.
HARTSFIELD, Richard 22.
HARTLEY, John 42.
HARVEL, Frederick 42(w). Chas. 15.Harvey
" 15, Harriett 42. Henry 42. Letty 42.
" Oliver 42. Richard 42. Watson 42.Wm.42.
HARWELL, Frederick 51. Jenny 51.Zimly 51.
HARWOOD, Thomas 21,40.
HAWKINS, Frances 42. James 31,34.
" Nicholas 31,34. Polly 42. Richard 42.
HAWTHORNE/HATHORNE, Andrew 61. Saml 56.
" William 61.
HAY, Samuel 5,14,44,62,63. Wm. 40.
HAYNES, Anthony 2. Thomas 2.
HAYNIE, Geo. 3,28,59. Margt. 3,59.
" Wilkins 52.
HAYS/HAYES, Geo. 4(w),55,60. James 41.
" 42. John 40,51. Jonothan 12,21,40.
" Louisa 41. Mary 41. Nancy 41.
" Rebecca 41. Sarah 41. Sophia 41.
" Samuel 21. Thos. 41,55.

HEAD, Daniel 1,40. Eliza 1. Wm. 1,34,40,
" 46.
HEADEN, Allen 36. Eli 35,36. Geo. 35(w),
" 36,37,62. Jane 35. Jesse 35. John 36.
" Prissy 36. Robert 35. Wm. 4,11,35(w),
" 36. Elizabeth 36.
HEARD, Abram 39. Chas. 13,38. Daniel
" 13,38. Eliza 13(w) 38. John 13,20,49.
" Joseph 24. Mary 13,38. Rachael 24.
" Richard 38(w). Sarah 24. Wm. 24(w).
" William Jr. 39.
HEARN, Betsy 20.
HEATH, Mourning 37. Richard 37.
HEMMING, Geo. 15,56,61.
HEMPHILL, Cynthia 50. Eliza 22,50.
" Esther 50. H. 20. James 6. Mary 50.
" Phillip 50. Robert 5. Sabry 5.
" Samuel 22. Thomas 32,49.
HENDERSON, Andrew 12,46(w),49. Chas. 16,
" Clementia 49. David 6(w),24.
" Delilah 6,7. Elias 6,7. Flora 46.
" Hannah 6,35,43. James 12,29,43,49(w),
" 50. Jeremiah 6. John 6,7,12(w),46.
" Joseph 17. Josiah 25(w). Margt. 12.
" Nathaniel 7. Rebecca 12. Robert 6,
" 10,27,59. Roxanna 25. Samuel 7(w),
" 10,16,31,37,43. Tabitha 6. Thomas 8.
" Wm. 42,46,48.
HENDLEY/Henley, Edmond 54. Geo. 14.
" Jane 4. Wm. 4. W. 40.
HENDON, Elijah 9,32,34. Isham 9,32.
" Patience 9.
HENDRIX/HENDRICKS, Berry 53. Fennel 53(w)
" Hannah 64. James 9,11,16,17,18,44,53,
" 59,63. Moses 53. Sarah 53. Thos. 53.
" Hillory 16.
HENNING?/HEMMING, Geo. 33
HENSON, John 33,61. J. 22.
HERRING/HERRIN, David Jr. 60. Moses 44.
HEWETT, Eliza 35. Ezekiel 51. Wm. 61.
HICKMAN, Jacob 37. Josiah 37. Lucretia 37.
" Nathaniel 37. Theopolius 28,37. Wm.37(w),
" 65.
HICKS/HIX, Nathaniel 51.
HICKSON/HIXON, Elizabeth 3. Rachael 35.
" William 3.
HIGGANBOTHAM, J. 26
HIGHTOWER, Thomas 29,31,38.

INDEX

HILL, Abraham 12. Edward 65. Isaac 16,17,
" 23, 30,33,45. James 28. John 29,31.
" Joshua 65. Theopolius 12. Thomas 1,9,
" 12,30. Wm. 51.
HILLHOUSE, David 15,40. D.44.Thos.40.
HINER, Abraham 18,19. Edwin 18. Jacob 18,
" 19. John 18. Lewis 18(w). Nancy 18.
HINES, Joseph 56.
HINTON, P.F. 48,49,52. Sally 26.Wood 19.
" P.F. 51.
HOBBS, Oliver 51
HITCHCOCK, James 54. Jesse 32. Wm. 32,
HOBBS, Oliver 51.
HOBBY, Wm. 21, 33.
HOBSON/HOPSON, Agnes 5. Allen 5. Baker 44.
" Christopher 5. Francis 5. John 4,44.
" Matthew 5,44. Nicholas 5(w),44. Patsy 5.
" Polly 5. Sally 5. Wm. 5.
HODGE, James 51(w). Jenny 51. Nancy 51,64.
" Thadeus 51. Wm. 31,31.
HODGES, Enoch 1.
HOGAN, Amanda 48. Frances 20. John 37.
" Nancy 20. Shadrack 48,52.
HOLDEN, Thomas 22.
HOLLAND, John 19,54. Lucretia 37. Meeky
" 19. Sewel 28. Thos. 57.
HOLLIDAY. Adolphus 53. Ambrose 11.
" Beatrice 53. Fanny 3,62. Francis 53.
" Jeremiah 3,4,9,53,62,63,64. John 3,
" 62. Julia 53. Margt. 9,59. Mariah
" 54. Martin 3,62,63. Nancy 3,62.
" Robert 53(w). Walton 53.
HOLLINGSWORTH, Volentine 43,59,62.
HOLMES, Alexa 47. Ann 4,63. Caroline 47.
" David 47(w). Henry 47. James 4.
" John 32,47. Marion 4. Mary 4. Sara 47.
" Sophronia 4. Wm. 47. Vivian 47.
" Washington 47.
HOLT, Harmon 44. Hines 1. Robert 1.
HOOD, Harriett 13. S.R. 41.
HOOKS, Betsy 37.
HOOPAUGH, James 51.
HOOPER, Nancy 19.
HOOVER, Jacob 33.
HORNSBY, Francis 2. Nancy 2.
HOPKINS, Aaron 54. Bethesda 54. Elijah 44.
" John 33. Richard 31. Samuel 44,46.
" Wm. 1,12,28,39,33,55,60.
HOPSON, Francis 19.

HORTON, Feraby 6. Fletcher 6. Jesse 42.
" John 27. Mary 49. Prosser 6(w),12,27,
" 37. Sarah 6. Wm. 6.
HOSCH, Henry 47,51.
HOUSE/HOWSE, Amanda 13. Ann 13. Caroline 13.
" Charlotty 13. Eliza 13. Frances 13.
" John 13,19,50.
HOWARD, Aquilla 3. Eliza 65. Hannah 8.
" Hardy 8,52(w),65. Hartsford 52. Harper 52.
" Homer 47,52. Jesse 47. John 47,52.
" Malinda 47. Samuel 52. Sara 8(w).
" Virgil 47, 52.
HOWELL, Wm. 15.
HUBBARD, Gabriel 29,30. John 16. Zenus 19.
HUBER, Isaac 21,40.
HUDDLESTON, Robert 55.
HUDSON, David 64. Lamech 74. Noah 55.
" Thomas 29. William 64.
HUGHES, Joseph 60. Robert 57,60. Thos.37.
HUGHEY, David 46. Eliza 46. Jas.38.
" John 46. Joseph 46(w).Mary 46. Susan 46.
HUMPHRIES, Geo. 29,58,59,61,62,63,65.
" John 37. Joseph 17,21,22,23,32,58,59,63,
" 65. J. 31. Shadrack 58,62. Uriah 21,59,
" 63. Wm. 29.
HUNNICUTT, Edmond 19.
HUNT, Esther 35. Moses 55. Thos. 34.
" William Jr. 34.
HUNTER, Betsy 19. D. 14. Geo. 1. Wm.48,53.
HUTCHINS, Malissa 51. Meredith 50.
HUTCHINSON/HUTCHERSON, Mary 25,66. Wm.
" 30,38,56,60.
HYDE, Robert 4,58. Thos 4,58,59,61,62,65.
HYNDS. John 38.

IRVIN, Lewis 14.

JACK, Eliza 65. John 34,60. Mary 34.
" P. 15. Thomas 60. Wm. 46.65.
JACKSON, Ephraim 13,14,42,52. Robert 15,45.
" Stephen 53.
JARRETT, Ann 8. Archelius 27,39. Delmas 52.
" Daniel 64. Howell 58,50,60,63,64. James 36.
" Martha 27. Nathaniel 58,59,64. Nicholas 36,
" 65. Oran 25. Patsy 65.
JELTON/JETTON, Jane 57. Joel 5,57. Margt. 5.
JENKINS, Edmond 2. Jesse 30.
JEPSON, Benj 56.
JOHNS, Bartlett 36,60. Martha 36. Phoebe 36.

VIII

INDEX

JOHNSON, Barnabas 26. Daniel 5,6,9,17,
" 44. Eliza 52. E.M. 50. Henry 24,64.
" James 25,46. Jasper 45. Joel 46.
" John 25,26,32,46. J.C. 48. Josiah 49.
" Martha 17. Mary 6,48. Nathan 64,65.
" Phoebe 19. Robert 4. R.D. 20. Sanford
" 52(w). Stephen 6. Thomas 6(w),13,24,
" 25,26,30,35,49(w). Wm. 6,12,33.
JOHNSTON[check Johnson], Elisha 32.
" John 20,25. Martha 25. Samuel 2.
JONES, Abner 34. Abraham 45,53. Basil 2,
" 16. Benj 59. Dudley 19. Elias 2.
" Eliphalet 38. James 14,19,43. Jane 14(w)
" John 25,32. Jonothan 32. Lewis 19.
" Malachi 27. Mary 9,43. Russell 6,19(w),
" 24,33,41,43,55. R. 64. Sophia 24.
" Thomas 9,19. Wm. 19,39,64.
JUSTUS/JUSTICE, Allen 18,41. Betsy? 18.
" David 20(w). Elvira 18. Henry 18,57.
" James 18. John 18(w). M.A.41. Polly 57.
" Sarah 20. Stephen 18. Thirsa 18.
" Wm 18,20,57.

KEIGLE, Roger 60.
KEITH, Elihu 16.
KELOUGH, Allen 28. Daniel 29. David Sr.
" 31. David Jr. 31. David 27,29,30,31.
" James 29,30. Jane 9. John 9. Mary 31.
" Thomas 31.
KEMP, Aaron 47. Malinda 47.
KENDRICK, Betsy 47. Forsythia 47.
KENNEDY, Josiah 25,33,61. Joshua 33.
" Rhoda 20. Sarah 61.
KENERLY, Geo. 26. John 30. Thos. 26.
KERBOW, Francis 50. Jesse 50. John 50.
" Sheila 50. Singleton 50. Solomon 50(w).
KEY, Ann 9,14,42. Geo. 12. James 12.
" John 12. Tandy 9,12(w). Thos. 12.
KEYTENDALE, James 37.
KIDD, Christopher 52. James 65. Marthy
" 50. Thomas 50,52. T.J.52.
KIMBERLY, Christopher 14.
KINERLY, John 29.
KING, David 13. Eleanor 38. Eliza 14,18.
" James 13. James Sr.13(w). John 13,14(w)
" 27,28,30,39,45. J. 45.
KINNEBREW, John 27.
KINNEY, Chas. 57.
KINSEY/KINZY, David 9, 17.

KINSEY/KINZY, James 9,17. John 56.
KIRKLAND, Eliza 4,44,63.Wm.4,44,63.
KIRKPATRICK, James 29,30. John 47.
" Sally 5. Thomas 15,23,31,45,55,61,
KNIGHT, Matthew 12,22,34. Presly 58.
KNOX, Ann 9,11. Benj 1. David 11.
" Isaac 20. James 9,11,28,44. John 65.
" Margt. 25. Mary 8. Polly 11.
" Samuel 7,8(w), 16,27,29,31,65.
" Samuel Sr. 8.
KOKER/COKER, Eleanor 46.
KOLB, Harmon 53,56,65. Harrison 53.
" James 53,56,64,65. Jonothan 53,56,
" 59 (will page 53), 63,64. Mary 53.
" Nancy 53. Peter 29. Polly 64.
" Rebecca 53,64. Richard 65. Sophia 53.
" Susannah 53,56,57,64.

LACEY, Wm. 26.
LAMAR, John 2. Lucy 2.
LAMB, Bethel 61.
LAMBERT, Edwin 6. John 6(w) Sara 6.
LAMPKIN/LAMKIN, Jeremiah 3. John 3.
" Lewis 8. Susannah 8.
LANCASTER, John 49.
LAND, Archer 17.
LANDERS, Eliza 19
LANDRUM, Eliza 51. Jackson 51. Jeptha 51.
" Joseph 6,51(w). Larkin 51. Sarah 51.
LANE/LAIN, John 39,59. Jonothan 9,44.
" Joseph 28.Sampson 39,54. Simeon 28.
LANGDON, John 16.
LANGFORD, Chatten 42. Allen 42, Wm.42(w).
" Willis 42.
LANGLEY, Oswell 64. Polly 64.
LANGSTON, James 25. John 3. Saml 24(w).
" James 53.
LAWHORN, A. 6.
LAWRENCE, Zachariah 38.
LAY, Ann 42. Caroline 42. Columbus 42.
" David 48. Elijah 48(w). Espy 51,. John 42.
" Larkin 48. Marcus 42. Martha 48. Mary 42.
" Richardson 42,48. Samuel 48. Wm. 42(w),48.
" Winney 42. Zachariah 25,64.
LEDBETTER, Buck 29. Eliza 48. Henry 32.
LEE, Cynthia 36. Jesse 53. John 44.
LEETH, Peter 1.
LEGG, James 26. Lucy 26. Nathaniel 26(w)
" William 26.

INDEX

LEON, Andrew 42. Nancy 42.
LESTER, Emily 50. Geo. 63. G.D.24.
" Josiah 50. Priscilla 63.
LEVINS, James 32. Richard 32.
LEWIS, Isham 6.
LIGHT, Obediah 17, 18.
LINDSEY, Abram 55. Abraham 15. Ephraim
" 31,45,53,59. Jacob 9,10,15,29,30,39,55.
" James 26,28,38. John 8,15,22,28,30,55.
" Josiah 55.
LIPHAM, A. 34. Frederick 22.
LIPSCOMB, David 47,52. Mina 47.
LITTLE/LIDDLE/LIDDELL, Andrew 26. A.J.50.
" David 56. James 26,56. Joseph 59,64.
" Margt. 50.
LITTLETON, Jacob 14,15. Milly 15.
LLEWELLYN, Wm. 57,60.
LOCKHART, Richard 40.
LOCKLIN, Samuel 53.
LOCKRIDGE, James 21.
LOFTIN, Nan 37.
LOLLY, Elisha 64.
LONG, Evans 16, 22. Henry 52. Nicholas 27.
" N/ 44.
LONGSTREET, Wm. 32.
LORD, Lucreta 51. Thos. 51. Wm. 51,52.
LOTT, Enoch 41. Geo. 41. Jane 41.
" Moses 41. Wm. 41(w).
LOVE, Sarah 37. Wm. 15.
LOVEJOY, Edward 4. Jemima 4. John 57.
" William 4.
LOW/LOWE, Fanny 38. James 46. Wm.38.
LOWRY, Frederick 7. James 7. John 7,42.
" Levi 5,20,42(w),43,58,59. Lin 64.
" Martha 34,42,48(w). Osborn 42. Sara 42.
" Willis 42.
LOYALL, Francis 18,45.
LOYD, William 23.
LUBBOCK, Richard 39.
LUCKIE, Jane 8. John 26,32,38. J.W.47.
" William F. 60.
LUKE, John 7.
LUMPKIN, Susannah 6.
LYLE/LILE, David 19. Eliza 19,50. George
" 4,44. Polly 20. Wm. 8,50.
LYNCH, Isaac 36. John 15,32,61.

McALPIN, Mary 54. Robert 22,29,54.
" Squire 31.
McCAIN, Thomas 31.
McCAMON, James 27.
McCAREL, Fanny 56.
McCARTER, Jeremiah 33.
McCARTNEY, Charles 27,28. John 28,32,55.
McCARTY, Cornelius 8,35,61,65. John 8(w).
" Mary 8,35. Wm. 18.
McCLAIN, Andrew 42. Jonothan 51
McCLESKEY, Ben 37. David 1,32,59,64.
" D.H.36. Eliza 7. Eusebius 7. James 7,18,
" 49,52(w),57,59. Madison 7. Margt. 7.
" Mary 7,32. Polly 7. Wm. 7.
McCOMMON, James 32. John 32. Margt. 32.
" Susannah 32.
McCONNELL, John 14,26,29,55,57.
McCORD, Abram/Abraham 10, 17. Esther 17.
" James 10. Nancy 10. Robert 10,28.
McCOY, Thomas 1.
McCRANEY, Robert 38.
McCRAVY/McCRARY, David 37,64. D.S,59,62.
McCREE, Benjamin 48. John 21. Wm. 21,27,
" 32,48.
McCULLARS/McCULLOUGH, David 43,57,58,64.
" Matthew 43. Ridley 43,57.
McCULLOCK, John 8,19,40,42,47,48. Mary 48.
McCURDY, David 35,63.
McCUTCHEON, James 39. John 32. Joseph 12,15,
" 22,23,26,27,28,29,34,37,39,45,53,54,55,56,
" 60,61. Patsy 18. Wm. 26,37,61.
McDANIEL, Josiah 54.
McDONALD, Chas. 27. James 3,35,63. John 20.
" Josiah 33,58,59,61,63. Mary 27.
McDOWELL, Allen 22. Margaret 24(w) Michael 22.
" Michael 22(w). Peggy 22.
McELHANNON, Christopher 7. Cooper 7. Eleanor 7.
" Frances 7,48. Hezekiah 48,51. Hugh 7,48,51.
" Isaiah 7. James 5. John Sr. 7(w). John 5,7,
" 26,59. Mary 48. Prunella 51. Sarah 48.
" Stewart 7,48. W.G. 51.
McELROY, John 31.
McEWING/McEwen, James 37. Martha 37.
McFALL, Dennis 33. Geo. 15,30,33,38,40.
" John 11,29,30,54.
McFARLAND, James 40. Mary 53.
McGARY, Edward 15
McGEHEE, Jesse 10,34. J. 33. Martha 34. Mial
" 34. Nathan 10,34(w). Osborn 34. Patsy 34.
" Robert 34. Solomon 34.

INDEX

McGILTON, Van. 61.
McGOVERN, Robert 27
McGOWAN, Edward 40. James 40(w). John 34,
" 40. Hamilton 40. Robert 29,31.
" Samuel 40.
McGRAW, John 34.
McGUIRE, Abner 6. Polly 41. Thomas 41.
McHARGUS, Alexa 63. Jas. 63. John 63.
McINTIER, Thomas 55.
McKEE, Lewis 27.
McKINSEY, Benjamin 50.
McKEY, Wm. 61.
McKINNEY, Charles 20(w),59. Chas.Jr.20(w)
" Eliza 20. Milda 20. Polly 20. Saml 20.
" Wilson 20,62. Wm. 20.
McLANE, Andrew 9.
McLAWS, Alexander 39.
McLEROY, Sarah 50.
McLESTER, Caroline 53. Cynthia 53.
" James 53. J.G.48,51. Jos. 53(w),63.
" Rhoda 53. Wm. 53. Jonothan 64.
McLURE, Moses 12.
McMILLEN(see McMullen), James 16,31,49,56.
" Peter 9,14,42.
McMULLEN, (see McMillen), James 27,
" Margt. 58,65. Samuel 58,65. Wm. 19.
McMURTY, Eliza 7.
McNAIR, David 62.
McNAUGHTON, Alexa 35.
McNEAL, Henry 24. John 24.

MACKEY/MACKIE/MACKEE, Mary 28. Thos. 28.
" William 38.
MADDOX, John 33. Joseph 20,37. Peter 26.
" William 1.
MAINS/MAIRS, Hugh 28,32,38. Jane 32.
" Nathaniel 28.
MALONE, John 28,29.
MANGUM/MANGRUM, Arthur 24. Eliza 47.
" Levina 47. William 47.
MANN, Henry 19. William 52.
MANSON, Ichabod 19.
MAPKIN, William 48.
MARBURY, Horatio 15,45. Leonard 2,4,14,
" 15,22,26,44.
MARCELLUS, Griffin 49.
MARCUS, John 1,53,56.
MARLER, Frances 51. Peterson 51.
MARLOW, Ramona 52.

MARRS, Hugh 22.
MARSHALL, John 2, Moses 2.
MARTIN, Elijah 19. Elisha 19,53. Jas.53,
" 54,55, John 1,19(w),34,55. Jonothan 38.
" Levi 19. Malachi 19. Mary 19.
" Matilda 59. Nancu 19. Philemon 31,34.
" Robert 37,62. Ruthy 19. Sarah 50.
" Simeon 19. Tabitha 59. W.D.24.
" Wm. D. 19,48,51,6 (48 is will)
MATTERSON, John 6.
MATTHEWS, Allen 20,46. Benj 46. Daniel 1,
" 28,33. George 22,54. Isham 27,33,60, 1.
" James 46. Jeremiah 31,32. John 22,49.
" Martha 46. Mary 20x, 46. Middleton 46.
" Nancy 20. Phineas 7,46. Roderick 13.
" Sarah 32. Wm. 6,46(w),54,64.
MAXWELL, David 2.
MAYFIELD, Battle 56,64.
MAY, Sterling 13.
MAYO, Benjamin 24(w). B.6. Sally 24.
" Rachael 47.
MELTON, Wm. 31.
MENAFEE, George 57.
MERCK, Henry 46.
MERIWETHER, Thomas 3.
MICHAEL, John 28.
MIDDLEBROOKS, Isaac 21,28,29,31.
MIDDLETON, Jack 14, John 21. Robt. 14.
MILLER, Andrew 23,28,29. Charity 7.
" Chas. 13. James 29,30. Jane 13.
" Jennett 25. Jerome 38(w). John 25(w),37.
" Mary 25. Sarah 48. Wm. 25,35,48,51.
MILLICAN/MILLIGAN, Andrew 24. Isaac 32.
" John 46. Moses 21,27. Robt. 42. Wm.32.
MILSAPS, Ezekiel 25. Fuller 25. Hiram 18.
" Jacob 25. John 18. Marvel 18,19.
" Mary 18. Thomas 25(w).
MILTON, John 56. Lucy 45. Wm. 45,54,56.
MINNISH, Agnes 51. Eliza 14,46,51,52(w).
" Franklin 46. Hardy 12. Isaac 51(w).
" John 46(w). Mary 46. Richard 46.
" Sidney 46.
MITCHELL, Giles 8,13,14,47,48,50,52.
" Hugh 53. James 7. Jane 50. Jesse 44.
" Jonothan 50. Mary 12. Thomas 6.
" Waler 20. Wm. 42.
MOBLEY, Eleazar 34. Elias 12. Jethro 4,34.
" John 35. William 53.
MOLDEN, John 60.

INDEX

MOLTON, Joseph 38.
MONTCASTLE, Ludwell 45.
MONTGOMERY, Bartlett 6. Hugh 5,6,24,29,36,
" 37,43,57,58,59,61,62,64. James 13,14,20,
" 24,58,59. Jane 49. J.M.C.58. Jas. 49.
" Masion 19. Mary 1. Robert 2.
MOOMAUGH, E.W. 41.
MOON, Archibald 8,13,24,41,52. Betsy 7.
" Bolar 7,13,42. B. 24. Eliza 7.
" Hartwell 7. Jackson 7. James 7,50.
" Jesse 42. John 13. Mary 51.
" Phillip 52. Robert 7, 24(w),47,50.
" Sally 7. Wm. 24.
MOONEY, Bryant 29,39. Hannah 3. Jos. 3.
" Mary 3. Uphe 37.
MOORE, Deborah 10, George 61,62. Jas. 9,
" 10,17,64. John 24,55,60. J. 38.
" Martin 60. Michael 9,17. Richard 9,16,
" 17. Samuel 10. Wm. 22,24(w),28,29,34.
" Abednego 33. Ann 34.
MORELAND, Martha 12.
MORENS, John 12.
MORGAN, Asa 28. Blake 5. Esther 5,63.
" Jesse 5,63. Joice 5. Mahalia 5,63.
" Polly 4. Priscilla 5,44. Robert 4,39.
" Thomas 4,44,58,59,61. Wm. 5(w),44,62.
" 63.
MORRIS, Eliza 5. Henry 51(w). Jas. 8,46.
" Jesse 5. John 5(w),57,62. Nancy 10,58.
" Robert 61. Sally 5,58. Susannah 5,
" Zachariah 5.
MORRISON, Alexa 1,12,13(w),22,32,33.
" Alfred 13. A.W/ 14. Cicero 13.
" Edward 13. Horatio 13. Mary 13.
" Thomas 14.
MORROW, Wm. 21.
MORTON, Joel 28. Joseph 32. Josiah 32.
MOSS, John 16,29,31,45. Wm. 39.
MOTE, Jonothan 3. Vardy 64.
MOWERS, Elias 45.
MURPHY, Jesse 19.
MURRAN, James 40.
MURRAY, David 3. Mary 3. Wm.47.
MYERS, Jacob 14.

NAIL, Alexa 23, Ezekiel 23. Frances 23.
" Joseph 23. Judith 23. Kezziah 23.
" Obediah 23. Savoy 23.
NALL, John 29,30,31. Martin/or Mark 12.
" 21,28,29. M. 16,23,54. Richard 12.
NANCE, John 8. Sarah 6. Wesley 8.
NAPIER, Thomas 55.
NASH, Elijah 7. Gabriel 7,49. Hannah 49.
" James Sr. 7(w). James 7. Margt. 7,49(w).
" Martha 49. Mary 49. Nancy 49.
" Reuben 7,49. William 7.
NAYLOR, George 39,54,60. Polydore 60.
NEAL/NIEL/NEEL, Frances 10,17. John 17.
" Jos. 10,13,17,23. Julian 17. Patrick 55.
" Peggy 66. Ruth 66. Thomas 66(w).
" Savoy 23.
NELSON, Eleanor 10. Francis 10. John 10,
" 11,18. Samuel 26,32,60. Sylvester 63.
NETTLES, James 28.
NEWTON, Henry 52. Mary 35. Wm. 35(w).
NIBLACK(The will shown on page 14 is in
the name of Black. It should be Niblack)
NIBLACK, Amelia 14. Augustine 14,
" Caroline 14. Cynthia 14. Emily 52.
" Hugh 14,52. Margt. 14. Samuel 14.
" Thomas 14(w),36,64. Virginia 14.
NICHOLS, John 61. Julius Jr. 55. Nancy 21.
" Thomas 29. Wm. 5,16,21,27,62.
NICHOLSON, Ann 13(w).
NIMMONS, William 8.
NIX, Rebecca 13. Thomas 13.
NIXON, Henry 20. John 20. Susannah 20.
" Tapley 20. Travis 20(w). Wm. 20.
NOBLES, Ster(ling) 54. Stephen 29.
NORMAN, Carolina 38. Eliza 25,38,66.
" Joseph 25. Lewis 38.
NORTON, Joseph 45.

O'BRIEN, James 21.
OFFUTT, Ezekiel 15.
OGLETREE, A.B. 54. John 54.
OGLESBY, B.H. 46.
OLIVE, Anthony 30.
OLIVER, Andrew 52. Elijah 5,24,49(w).
" Mary 49. Peter 32. R.A. 41. R.E. 52.
ORR, Anderson 46. Easley 37. Jas. 25,37(w)
" 65. John 25. Martha 25. Nancy 25.
" Thos. 25

XII

INDEX

OTWELL, Wm. 11
OWEN/OWENS, David 57. Epraim 51. Sara 25.
" 66. William 32.

PACE, Agnes 26. R. 26. Wm. 29.
PARK[see Parks], Amanda 48. Andrew 14,51.
" Anna 50. Betsy 50. B.F. 8,51. E.45,54.
" Garrett 10,43. Hannah 8(w). Jas. 10.
" John 6,7,8,10,31,41,50. Peggy 50.
" Russell 8,49. R.J.47. Sally 10. Saml 33.
" William 33,50(w).
PARKER, Matthew 43. Sally 43.
PARKS[see Park], Aaaron 3. Garrett 3,11.
" G.W.64. James 33. Nancy 50. Robert 9,
" 11,33,50. Samuel 29,30. Sarah 3.
" William 49.
PARR, Benjamin 26,29,38.
PARSONS, Patsy 6. William 29.
PARTIN, John 16,21.
PATE, Cordy 15,55. Jesse 18.
PATRICK, Alexa 15. Ephraim 5. Jane 13.
" John 13,22,55. Luke 15. Mary 13.
" Millican 15. Paul 1,15,16,21,29,40,45.
" Robert 13. W. 54.
PATTERSON, Arthur 63. Josiah 63. Rhoda 18
" William 63.
PATTON, Arthur 21,30,32,39,56. John 15.
" Martha 31. Samuel 18,25(w),28,29,63.
" Thomas 54,56. William 56.
PAYNE, Edward 57. Moses 34,45,61.
" Thomas 14.
PAYTON, William 12,22,64[See Peyton]
PEACH, James 20.
PEAK, Candace 10. David 10. Judith 10.
PEARCE, Susannah 65. Willis 65.
PEARSON, John 22.
PENDERGRASS, Edwin 49(w), Eliza 49. John
" 49. N.H. 48,51,52. Patsy 18.
PENNINGTON, Jacob 28. John 44,62.
" Samuel 21.
PENTECOST, Delilah 4,35. Matthew 6.
" Rachael 6. Richard 19. Wm. 4,24,28,29,
" 35. W. 19, 24.
PERKINS, Constantine 65. Malissa 65.
" Sally. 65. Zeno 48,65.
PERRY, Ben 28. Eli 21. Isaac 33.
" James 21. Nathaniel 21. Thos. 5,57,58.
PERRYMAN, Jeremiah 45. J. 45.
PETTIJOHN, Abram 5. Betsy 5. Jacob 5(w),
" 43,60. James 5,50. Reuben 5.
" Temperance 50. Warren 5. Wm. 5.

PETTY, Adah 14(w). Alexander 14.
PEYTON[see Payton], Wm. 27.
PHARR[see Parr] Edward 18,20. Francis 10.
" Hezekiah 20. Jonotha n 10,35.
PHELPS, Glen 6. Harriett 12.
PHILLIPS, Adam 20. Edward 29,56. Eliza 20.
" Geo. 55. Henry 20. Jasper 54. Jean 21.
" Jenny 12,40. John 20. Levi 20.
" Polly 6. Samuel 12. Thomas 20(w).Wm.39,
PIERCE, Tabitha 36. Wiley 38.
PINSON, Amy 59. James 59. Jos. 59.
" Susannah 59. Wm. 37,53.
PINKSTON, Daniel 17.
PITTMAN, A.B. 52. Cynthia 41. Geo. 50.
" James 9,16,17,18,22,27,28,29,30,35,38,
" 48,55,60,64. John 20,64. J. 16,27.
" J.O. 51. Milly 50. M.H.25. Noah 41.
" P.A. 8. Sally 50. W.J.48.
POLK, Cillar 6. Sally 6.
PONDER, John 27.
POOL, Adair 44. Alice 26. Bathena 26.
" Drury 26. John 26. Lania 26. Polly 26.
" Samuel 26(w), 50. Seymour 26.
POPE, Burwell 34,53,55. Elijah 15.
" John 26. Priscilla 55. Willis 38,57.
PORTER, Benjamin 55. James 29.
POTTS, Alexa 8. Caroline 52. Cicero 41.
" Eliza 41. Henry 41(w),31. Mary 8,20.
" Moses 8,40,41,52. Sarah 48. Stephen 6.
" Thomas 8. Unity 7,41. Wm. 8(w),11,38,
" 56, 65.
POULSON, Jane 35. Jonothan 4. Mark 4,44,61.
POWELL, Abraham 6. Oliver 19.
POYNER, George 65.
Poythress[POYTHRESS] John 15.
PREWETT/PRUITT, Hezekiah 24,25. Jno. 53.
PRICE, Daniel 27,39,40. E. 6. James 16,
" Thomas 32.
PRICHETT, Sion 6,38
PRICKETT, John 47. Polly 47.
PRINCE, Oliver 34.
PULLMAN, James 27.
PURKERSON, Beverly 65.
PURYEAR, Rebecca 39. Wm. 18,31,39.

QUELLY, William 32.

INDEX

RAGAINS, John 5.
RAINEY/RAMEY, Absolom 16,21,23,27,28,29,
" 55. Ann 55. A. 16,60. John 29,55. Wm.54.
RAKER, John 39./R61
RALSTON, Ezekiel 4,57,62.
RAMSEY, Catey 11. Eliza 44. E.A.46.
" Henry 44,62. James 11. Robert 3.
" William 44,46.
RANDOLPH, Elijah 52. Eliza 49,52.
" Hilliard 51,52,14. H.J. 48. John 7,52.
" Joshua 49. J.H.51,52. Martha 52.
Mary 52. Tandy 51. Washington 7,52.
" Wood 49,52(w). W.L.O.52.
RASBERRY, Mary 19.
RATCHFORD, James 20. Joseph 9,11,17,20,(w)
" 42,59,60. Polly 6,20. Robert 20,42(w).
" Joseph 20. Ezekiel 20.
RAY, David 31. Geo. 46,56. Solomon 46,56.
REED, David 40. Isaac 4. Jos. 35.
" Stephen 59.
REEVES, Jeremiah 14,24.
REINTZELL, Daniel 22.
RENCH, John 33,45.
REYNOLDS, Amanda 18. Chas. 3, Harmon 28.
" John 18,29,30,47,61. Joshua 49. Mary 3.
" Thomas 23,28. Travis 18. Wm. 18(w).
RHEA, Betsy 24.
RICE, Benjamin 21,23,55. Jeremiah 56.
" William 55,56.
RICHARDSON, John 21.
RICKETSON, T. 3.
RIDEN, Benj. 49(w). Caleb 7,49. Elijah
" 49. John 25,49.
RILEY, Edward G. 50.
ROBERSON, ROBERTS, ROBERTSON, ROBISON,
" Alcy 7(w), David 31,36. Edmond 37.
" James 36. John 7(w),34,38,56. Mary 8.
" Rebecca 20. Terrell 25. Thomas 45.
" William 14,30,32,34,54.
ROBY, Elijah 37.
ROGERS, Arminta 41. Benj. 4,64,54. David
" 5,17,36,58,59,63,65. Dempsey 54.
" Eliza 25. Enoch 50. Frances 25,66.
" Franklin 48. George 42. Jacob 50.
" James 5,20,23,35,36,44,48,58. Job 5.
" John 5,16,17,23,32(w),38,48(w),50(w).
" 58,62,63. Joseph 25. Martha 9,16,17,
" 32. Mary 5,16,17,25. Milly 63.
" Nancy 25,50,66. Obedience 16.

ROGERS, continued
" Peleg 5,9,17,43,44,56. Polly 25,50,58.
" 63. Rhoda 20(w). Sarah 25,48.
" Theoploius 20. Unity 4,54. Thos. 4,5,
" 9,16,17,25,29,32,43,44,45,48,50,58,59.
" 63. Wm. 25, Zilla 63.
ROLLING, Permelia 50.
ROSE, Mary A. 14.
ROSS, Thos. 40. Wiley 3,4,62
ROSSAU, John 15.
ROSSON, John 32.
ROUDEN, Rhoda 20.
ROWE, James 49.
ROWLAND, Eleshba 38.
RUDLING, Sally 50.
RUNNELLS, Preston 61.
RUNNOLDS, Howell 34.
RUSHTON, John 57.
RUSSAU, Wm. 45.
RUSSELL, Jacob 15. Thomas 60.
RUTLEDGE, Thomas 22.
RYAN/RIAN, Jane 8. Obedience 6,8(w).
" Phillip 14(w),8. Phillip Sr. 6(w).
" Rachael 14. Whitehead 8.
RYLIE, Bennett 49.

SAILORS, Abner 7.
SANDRETH, Moses 31.
SATTERFIELD, Wm. 24.
SCISSION[see Sisson], Charlotte 5, Jas.5.
" John 5(w). Vardary 5.
SCOTT, Abram/Abraham 9,11,15,56.
" Andrew 64. Ann 12. Elizabeth 45. James
" 26,29. John 40,45. Joseph Sr. 38(w).
" Joseph 4,12,38,60,64. J. 24. Nancy 64.
" Susannah 12,38. Thos. 27,33,38,39.
SCREVEN, Thomas 35.
SCROGGINS, Benj 20. Catt 31. Charlton 29.
SEALS, John 31.
SEATES, Berrilay 14.
SEAY, John Sr. 49. Ransom 50. Sarah 6.
SEVENTYN, Leonard 27
SEXON, Solomon 42(w). Susan 42.
SHACKLEFORD, Jane 40. Richard 1.
SHADRACK, George 59
SHANKLE, Eli 12. James 42(w),51. Levi 52.
" Lucinda 42. Seaborn 42,47,48.
SHANNON, Thomas 31.
SHARKS, Brantley 12. Wm. 12,21.

INDEX

SHARP, Avilla 64. Edmond 50. James 15.
" Jane 50. Jarrell 50. Lewis 47,50.
" Marilla 50. Mary 47,50. Nathan 50(w).
" Noah 47(w),50. Russell 50. Wm. 1,46,50
" 64,65.
SHEARS, Moses 31. Rachael 35.
SHED, William 35,36.
SHAW, Arabella 8. Bryan 19. Delilah 26.
" Elijah 26. George 8,24,38. Jas. 19.
" Nathan 19. Permelia 19. Susannah 19.
" William 19(w),26.
SHEPPARD, John 34. Patsy 5. Providence 22.
SHIELDS, Betsy 58. Catey 38. Charity 13,
" 25. George 8,58. James 4,5,8,13,19,25,
" 43,44,57,58,62.Jane 4,44,61,62. John
" 19,29,45,58. Joseph 5(w),39,57,58,59.
" Josiah 44. Mary 13. Nancy 58. Patrick
" 4,43,44,57,60,61,62. Patsy 58,59.
" Peggy 5,7. Polly 58. Samuel 39,44.
" Thomas 4,39.
SHIPP, John 62. Martha 35. Sylvanus 26.
" William 4,35.
SHOCKLEY, Gideon 57. Thomas 19,57. Wm.43.
SHODDARD, John 21. Tabitha 21.
SHORT, Jonas 32.
SHOTWELL, Jesse 20,46.Nathaniel 20,26,46,
" 46(w). Rebecca 46.
SHRINER, Peter 60.
SIBBALD, George 56,61.
SIDWELL, David Jr. 26.
SIMMS, James 33. John 26. Michael 28.
SIMONTON, Thomas 46.
SIMPKINS, Benj 66. John 52. Wm. 66.
SIMPSON, Rice 31
SINGLETON, John 7,8. Jos. 7,26.
SISSON[see Scisson], James 20,52. John 52.
SKINNER, John 26,42,59,65.
SLATON/SLATEN/SLAYTON, Fleming 5,65.
" Little B. 19. Mary 43,46,65. Munasa 49.
" Uriah 46(w), Waid 19. Wm. 49.Polly 65.
SMEDLEY, Thomas 45.
SMELLERS, Joseph 61.
SMITH, Alexa 28. Alford 13. Alfred 49.
" Anna 36. B. 33,40. Chas. 6,13,16,29.
" Claborn 20. Dianna 13. Eliza 13,16.
" George 32,53. Gideon 41. Green 14.
" Henry 7. David 7. Hezekiah 7. Israel 7.
" James 7,13(w),14,25,36(w),57,64. Jane
" 49. J. 33. Jimmy 5. John 27,28,29,36,
" 41,44,55,57,60,61,64. Lucy 16.

SMITH - continued
" Martha 13. Mary 41(w). Nancy 36.
" Nehemiah 63. Patsy 5. Payton 39.
" Polly 36,41. Ralph 61. Robert 56.
" Samuel 36,41. Silas 36. S.M.8.
" Wm. 7,28,36,41,42. W.S. 15.
SMITHWICK, Robert 20.
SMYTHE, Thomas Jr. 2.
SNOW, Eliza 5, Henry 5(w),58. Mark 5.
" Moses 5.
SORRELLS, Charles 19,54.
SPARKS, Jeremiah 22. Jesse 12,60.
" Matthew 12. Uriah 25.
SPEARS, Absolom 25. John 17. Moses 56.
SPENCE, Nancy 19.
SPIERS, John 22,23.
STALLINGS, James 12.
STAMPS, James 9,10. Timothy 9,10.
STAPLER, Amos 25,26. A.D. 41. John 46,
" 48,66. Mary 41. Robert 25,41(w),66.
" Ruth 66(w),25. Sarah 41. Thos. 8,
" 25(w),41,46,48,49,50,52,66.
" Thos. Jr. 25. Thos. Sr. 46,47.
" William 25,50,66.
STATLER
STEED, Carlton 51. Fanny 25. Green 25.
STEELE, Alex 3. Fanny 3.
STEPHENS, Benj 38. Solomon 5,58.
STEPHENSON, William 22.
STEWART, Clements 54. Eliza 49.
" James 21,29,31. J. 15. Mary 49(w).
" Richard 49. Samuel 65. Sarah 49.
STILES, John 39.
STINSON, William 29,30.
STOCKTON, Benjamin 50(w) Eliza 50.
" James 50, Sarah 50. Thirza 50.
STODDARD, John 27.
STOKES, Nancy 27. Wm. 12,22,27,32,39,
" 61.
STONE, Jenny 61. Matthew 12,27,60,61.
" William 21,55,66.
STONEHAM, Eliza 37. Erastus 37. Geo. 37.
" Henry 37(w). James 37. Jane 37. John 37.
" Joseph 37. Martha 37. Mary 37. Sophia 37.
" Susannah 37. Wm. 37.
STORY, A.G. 7,50. Caroline 52. Christian 5.
" Cynthia 50. Edward 5,8,21. James 21,52.
" Thomas 5(w).

INDEX

STOVALL, Benj 57. Emily 14. Harriett 14.
" Jeptha 14. Julia 14. John 14(w),
" Manor 49. Margt. 14. Mariah 14,
" Martha 14. Mary 14. Prudence 36. Wm.14.
STRANGE, James H. 40.
STRAWBRIDGE, Lydia 20.
STREET, Dorcas 8. Polly 8,41. Samford 8.
" Samuel 8(w),57,63,65. S.R. 14. Wm.8.
STREETMAN, Wm. 32.
STRICKLAND, Bethany 41. Carless 48.
" Chas. 10. Clement 59. Eliza 56(w),59.
" Ezekiel 35. Hardy 14,52,57,58,59,62.
" Henry 10,26,58,59,62,64. H. 56.
" Isaac 59. Jacob 26. John 48,56. Mary
" 26. Nancy 59. Rachael 66. Samuel 41.
" Solomon 11,35,55. Wm .64. Wilson 59,62.
STRINGER, James 30. John 60.
STRONG, Isham 1,9,22,39,45. John Sr. 16.
" John 60. Johnson 1,55. Wm. Jr. 45.
" Wm. Sr. 22,45. Wm. 1,12,15,16,22,26,29,
" 39,45,54,55.
STROTHER, Eliza 23. Frances 27. Jane 23.
" Margt. 39, Peter 39. Wm. 23.
STROUD, John 1.
STUART, James 18.
STUBBLEFIELD, Ann 11.
STUBBS, Isaac 61.
STURGIS, Daniel 2.
STYLES, Sarah 6.
SUMMERALL, Henry 9, 10.
SUMMERFORD, Jacob 10,11.
SUMMERLIN, Jacob 29.
SUMMERS, John 22. Nancy 19.
SUTTON, Eliza 8. Henry 64.
SWAIN, James 37.
SWAN, Lemuel 13.
SWEPSON, John 45.
SYMES, John 27.

TABBS, Isabelle 13. James 13.Lewis 13.
" William 13.
TAIT/TATE, Delilah 8,19. James 8(w),47,59
" Mary 8,19. Susannah 8,19.
TALIAFERRO, Benjamin 22.
TAPP, Charles 6.
TARBOROUGH, Stephen 59.
TATUM, Luke 16,22.
TAYLOR, Champion 9,21. Daniel 10,33.
" Edmond 28,33,55. Geo. 15,27,31,32,33,
" 45.

TAYLOR, Grant 15. James 14. Wm. 45.
TELFAIR, Governor 1.
TEMPLETON, John 55.
TERRELL, David 45. Hezekiah 1.
" Peter 61. Thos. 1,61. Will 45.
THOMAS, Christiana 37,58. David 19.
" Frederick 60. Giles 26. Hannah 26.
" James 11,27,31,32. Jett 18,30. S.Jr.14.
" William 58.
THOMASON, Gideon 35.
THOMEY, George 42.
THOMPSON, Abraham 61. Andrew 57.
" Frederick 5,57. Green 40. Hugh 19.
" Jesse 36,40. John 1. Lewis 40.
" Mourning 40. Sherrod 40(w). Wm. 40.
" W.S. 49.
THORNTON, Benajah 41,53. Eliza 48. Mark 54.41(w)
" Mary 41. Polly 47. Prior 16. Stephen 12,41.
" S.A. 48.
THRASHER, Joseph 46.
THURMOND, Absolom 16,45. Andrew 41. Anglin 41.
" Belton 8. Charles 16,45. Christopher 41.
" Elisha 52. Eliza 51. George 41. Harris 62.
" Harrison 9,14,41(w). James 41,54,63.
" Jane 5,9,14,41,42. Jeferreson 50. Jenett 41.
" Jesse 41. John 9,16,17,41,45. Mandolin 41.
" Martha 52. Mary 52. Nancy 63. Permely 52.
" Phillip 44. Richard 17. Sarah 41. Susannah
" 8. Thomas 5,51,58,59,62. Troup 41.
" William 7,16,17,41,45,52(w). Willis 58,62.
TIDWELL, Absolom 29. Isaac 29. Job 28.
" Peter 29. Wm. Sr. 28. Wm.Jr. 28.
TIGNER, Phillip 54.
TILLMAN, Dickson 43. James 46.
TINDELL, John 1.
TINDLEY, Thomas 45.
TITSMOUTH, Isaac 13(w).
TODD, John 6.
TOLBERT, James 13. Levi 41. Matthew 16.
TOWNS, John 33.
TOWNSEND, Henry 37. Solomon 37. Thos.37.
TRAPP, Sally 6.
TRAYLOR, Champion 12. Randall 12. Randolph
" 21,28,29,34.
TREADWELL, Isaac 31. Rachael 19.
TRENT, Henry 29.
TRIPLETT, William 61.
TROUP, Madison 12
TROUT, Nathaniel 43. Sara 8(w).

INDEX

TRUCE, Brandrick 56
TRUETT, Purnell 39
TUCKER, Robert 31
TULLY, David 44.
TURK, John 41. Nancy 41.
TURNER, Butler 43. Carrie 43. Henry 36.
" James 36. John 34,45,53. Sally 43,57.
TUTTLE, David 5. James 56. Jas. Jr. 29.
TYLER, James 42. William 26.

UPTON, Sally 55.

VANN, James 44,58,62.
VARNER, George 22. Matthew 22.
VARNUM, Asa 7,8,20,26. Anna 7. James 50.
" William 7.
VENABLE, Abraham 3,4. Absolom 62.
" Charles 6,43. Frances 10. Isabelle 19.
" James 42,46. John 25,42,52. Mary 46.
" Nathaniel 25. Robert 10,19(w),25.
" Samuel 46. Sarah 42.
VERMILLION, Benjamin 21,22,23.Tabitha 21.
VINSON, Elizabeth 8. George 8,12,18.
" Martha 18. Moses 12,18,25. Wm. 41.

WADE, J.H. 53,46.
WADSWORTH, John 57. Sally 57. Sarah 63.
" Seaborn 57. Thos. 57. William 57.
WAFER, Asenith 19. James 19. Thos.19,63.
WAGGONER, Wm. 45.
WAGNON, John 15,38.
WAITS, William 59,62.
WAKEFIELD, Charles 9,10.
WALKER, Augustus 41. Bartlett 37.
" Christian 35. Elethen 35. Eliza 41(w).
" Henry 3,35(w),45. John 35.
" Jonothan 35. Nathaniel 41. Wm.35,54.
WALL, Benjamin 53.
WALLACE[see Wallis], Eady 24. Hannah 20,
" 61. James 53. John Sr. 14. John 14,20,
" 61. Mary 20. Rachael 19(w).
" Thompson 24. William 39.
WALLER, Joseph 55.
WALLING, Hannah 24. Lucy 24. Michael
" 24(w). Priscilla 24. Rachael 24.
" Thomas 24.
WALLIS[see Wallace], Daniel 24. Isaiah
" 24. Jenny 24. John 24. Josiah 18.
" Levi 24(w). Margt. 24. Thompson 24.
" William 24.

WALTON, John 22. Nevill 27. Robt. 56,61.
" Thomas Jr. 15. Thomas 22.
WARD, Thomas 56,57,64.
WARREN, Abraham 31.
WATES, William 43[see Waits]
WATKINS, Jane 52. John 5,52(w),57.
" Luke 52. Wm. 30,33,50,61.
WATSON, Anderson 54. Benj 17,24. Jos.6.
" Josiah 5. Martha 51. Nancy 7.
" Obediah 6(w). Samuel 40,42,44,48.
" Sarah 17,23,35. Thomas 44,56,64.
WATTEROUR, Kizziah 19.
WATTERSON, John 4,60.
WATTS, Benjamin 45,63. Richard 36.
WAUGH, Eliza 22. Harrison 22. Jas. 24.
" Susan 22.
WAY, John Jr. 26.
WEATHERBY, George 55,61.
WEATHERFORD, Archibald 37. Chas.37(w),63.
" Charity 37.
WEBB, Amanda 52. Eliza 34,48,52. Horatio
" 9,20,36,42. H. 12,22,25.John 33,34.
" J.O. 52. Rachael 20. Thos. 28.
" Wilborn 20. Willis 20,51.
WEBSTER, John 14. Moses Sr. 14. Sarah 3/
WEIR, John 46. Patton 45.
WELBORN, A.T. 51. Cobb 51. Curtis 17,27.
" Elijah 54. Eliza 51. Innes 51. James 51(w)
" John 51. M.H. 51. Simeon 51. Wm. 7,51.
WELLS, Benjamin 2. Ezekiel 21,54,56.
" Samuel 21.
WEST, Henry 27. Sarah 18. Wm. 1.
WHALEY, Eli 59. 5.
WHATLEY, Taylor 36.
WHEELER, Charity 48. Daniel 48. John 48.
" James 48(w).
WHITE, Daniel 38. Geo. 22. Medley 38.
" Robert 14,56,51. Sally 60. Simeon 37,63, 6
" Thomas 34. Ann 40.
WHITEHEAD, E. 47.
WHITEMORE, Tamar 37.
WHITLOCK, Polly 57.
WHITNEY, James R. 14,15,27,33,34,45,55,56,61
" John R. 45. Polly 45.
WHITSELL, George 61.
WHITTEN, Robert 3.
WHITWORTH, Jacob 36(w),57. Samuel 36,57.
WHORTON, Benjamin35,37. William 37.

INDEX

WILBANKS, Ann 47. Richard 13. Wm. 47.
WILDER, E. 47.
WILEY, Matthew 5. Peter 55. Wm. 65.
WILHITE, Meshack 8. M.T. 13,14,20.
WILKERSON, Susannah 12.
WILKES, Simeon 14.
WILKINS, Samuel 26.
WILLIAMS, Butler 7. Daniel 39,45. Edward
" 27, 31. Isaac 4. Isham 27. Jas. 8.
" John 61. Littleberry 15. Polly 4,45.
" Robert 28. Thomas 40. W.H. 50.
WILLIAMSON, Adam 7. Alexa 25. A.J. 48.
" John 46,48. J.P. 48. Micajah Sr. 4,
" 46,60,61. Micajah Jr. 4,34,60.
" Micajah 1,16, 18(w),21,22,23,30,39,
" 45,54,55,56. M. 34,56,60. Peter 56.
" Polly 18,39,55. Rachael 24. Richard
" 2,13. Sally 60. Susannah 56. Wm.7(w),
" 15,18,21,61.
WILLINGHAM, Eliza 12. Fanny 46.
" Harriett 12(w). Jesse 46,61. Thos.35.
WILLIS, James 41. John 49. Wm. 3.
WILLS, Abner 13,49. Cicero 49. Edward 14.
" Eliza 49. Ezekiel 27. James 49.
" Jos. 49. Leander 49. Martha 49.
" Martin 49. Sarah 49. Thomas 49(w).
WILSON, Benjamin 18. Boley 14. Caroline
" 6. Dicey 49. Fanny 64. Fennell 49.
" Geo. Sr. 18(w). Geo. Jr. 29. Geo. 18,
" 28,29. Henry 49. Isaiah 49. Jas. 9,
" 18,25,35. Jane 6,49. John 6,9,12,18,
" 35,39,49,54. Joshua 50. Lucy 6. Lydia
" 6. Mary 6,49. Michael 49(w). Moses 14.
" Nancy 25. Phenail 43. Polly 25.
" Rebecca 25. Rhody 49. Robert 18,55.
" Samuel 6,61. Susannah 49. Thos.25(w).
" William 6,18,49.
WIMBERLY, James 17. John 17. Sarah 7.
WINDZOR, Jesse 50.
WINN, Elisha 9,12,14. Judith 9,14,42.
WINTERS, Angeline 50. A.J.48. Charity 25.
" Eliza 66. G.W.66. John 18(w),25,66.
" Nancy 18. Richard 66(w). Susan 66.
" Wm 13,18,42,50(w)
WITT, Charles 41,42,53. David 24,43,44,
" 51,56,65. Martha 42. Middleton 42,48,
" 51(w),52. M. 25. Sarah 51.
WOFFORD, Absolom 20(w),42,64. Eliza 20.
" James 48. John 20,42. Moses 42.

WOOD/WOODS, C.W. 47. Eliza 47. Ethelred
" 11,29,35,57. Frances 7,47. Green 57.
" G.B. 51. James 7,36,47,50,60. John 7,
" 29,31,34,50. Josiah 1,12,33. Lourena
" 48. Melton 47(w). Polly 36,50. Sally
" 33,35. Susannah 50. Wm. 7,43,47(w),50.
WOODROUGH, Richard 27.
WOODWARD, Francis 31.
WOOTEN, John 1. Tabitha 26,27.Thos.Jr.
" 44. Thomas 26,27,32,44,45,46.
WORSHAM, H. 51.John 51. Ludwell 8,51(w).
" Nancy 51. R. 26,39,40. Wynne 51.
WRAY, Geo. 34.
WRIGHT, Alsy 2,24,35,57,59. Cassandra 57.
" Cassey 35. Cornelius 35,59. Elias 24,
" Hannah 35. Hawkins 50. Henry 3.
" Issac 4,57,62. Isaiah 2. James 1,3,57.
" John 2,35(w),57,58,59. Martha 57.
" Nathan 26. Patsy 35. Reek 35. Rhoda 24.
" Sally 35.
WYATT, Hannah 34. John 32. Mary 32.
" Payton 22,34. Richard 29.

YARBROUGH, Ambrose 37,57.
YORK, Isaac 6.
YOUNG, John 6. William 54.
YOUNGBLOOD John 3.

ZACHARY, Barthomolew 9,17. Wm. 2
ZIMMERMAN, Phillip 38.

XVIII

www.ingramcontent.com/pod-product-compliance
Lightning Source LLC
Chambersburg PA
CBHW030558080526
44585CB00012B/416